DO YOU KNOW WHAT YOU'RE EATING?

MAYBE NOT!

Approximately 70 percent of the foods we eat may contain genetically engineered components. And that number is growing! But what do we REALLY know about the impact of genetic engineering on our lives and our environment? The authors tackle many difficult questions: What is genetic engineering and what are genetically engineered foods? Should we eat these foods? Are they safe? Are they natural? Are these foods the solution to world hunger or are they potentially damaging, containing myriad serious, unanticipated side effects and risks? The authors urge you to learn as much as you can about these issues so that you can protect yourselves, your families and the genetic heritage of the earth.

Genetically Engineered Foods

Are They Safe?
You Decide.

Laura Ticciati
and
Robin Ticciati, Ph.D.

K   P

NTC/Contemporary Publishing Group

The intention of *Genetically Engineered Foods* is solely informational and educational. The text was accurate at the time of publication. Because things change rapidly in this field we cannot guarantee that all statements will be correct when you read this book. Please feel free to contact Mothers for Natural Law for an update if you have any questions.

GENETICALLY ENGINEERED FOODS

Copyright © 1998 by Laura Ticciati and Robin Ticciati

Library of Congress Cataloging-in-Publication Data

Ticciati, Laura
    Genetically engineered foods : are they safe? you decide / Laura Ticciati and Robin Ticciati
       p.   cm.
    Includes bibliographical references (p.   ) and index.
    ISBN 0-87983-967-8
    1. Agricultural biotechnology.   2. Food-Biotechnology
3. Nutrition.   1. Ticciati, Robin.   II. Title.
S494.5.B563T53   1998
363.19'2 — dc21   98-8678
                                   CIP

Printed in the United States of America

Published by Keats Publishing
A division of NTC/Contemporary Publishing Group, Inc.
4255 West Touhy Avenue,
Lincolnwood (Chicago), Illinois 60646-1975 U.S.A.

Contents

Preface   *vii*
Introduction   *xi*

Chapter One: Genetic Engineering —
   Hopes and Hazards   1
   The Dangers of Genetically
      Engineered Foods   4
   What is Our Government Doing?   8

Chapter Two: Truth in Labeling?   15
   What's on the Market?   15
   A Ray of Light — Certifying   21
   Non-GE Infant Formula   22

Chapter Three: Science and Safety   24
   What is Science?   24
   Objective Science Provides
      Partial Knowledge   26
   Technology and Side Effects   28

Safety Comes with Experience   30
Genetic Engineering —
    Unpredictable and Unsafe   32
Genetic Engineering — Violation of
    Natural Law   37
Safety Testing of Genetically
    Engineered Foods   41
Genetic Engineering — A "What If?" Issue   44

Chapter Four: Biotechnology Claims   45
Claims Versus Facts   45
The Bottom Line   51

Chapter Five: What You Can Do   54
Overseas Efforts   54
What's Happening in America?   57
What is Mothers for Natural Law Doing about It?   58
Other U.S. Resources: Materials,
    Organizations, Action   62
How Did We Get Here?   67

Conclusion   70
Notes   72
About the Authors   75
Petition   77
Index   79

Preface

We first heard about genetic engineering from a friend — John Fagan. John is a molecular biologist who had been funded by the NIH for many years to conduct genetic engineering research in relation to cancer. For over twenty years, with grants totaling more than $2.5 million, that's what he did. Then in 1994, he decided to stop. He was disturbed by the direction in which biomedical research was heading, concerned that his work could be used for potentially dangerous applications and felt he had to tell people about it. So he returned over $600,000 to the NIH, withdrew his proposals for another $1.25 million, and launched a global campaign to alert the public about the hazards of genetic engineering.

We heard John speak in June 1996, and were stunned by what he said. One month later, our newly founded organization, Mothers for Natural Law, put everything else on hold and launched a national public awareness campaign on genetically engineered foods and a Consumer Right to Know Initiative for mandatory labeling. For nearly two years we have traveled across the country speaking with scientists, food industry members, farmers, government officials and consumers about the dangers of genetically engineered foods, working to awaken an appreciation for the significance of this new technology in our lives, and to promote financially viable, environmentally responsible solutions to the challenges this issue raises for all of us.

Genetic engineering has given rise to a storm of controversy. Some are messianic about its benefits. Others are violently opposed to it on every level. We cannot pretend not to have an opinion on the subject. Genetic engineering is one of those technologies that could compromise the integrity of life as we know it. It is not a back-burner issue. It is probably the largest nutritional experiment the world has ever seen, and we are the guinea pigs. We believe that genetically engineered foods must be taken off the market until they are proven safe for us and the environment, and until that happens, they must be labeled.

As a nation, we're always in a hurry. Quick, easy, cheap — these are the things most of us look for. It's our style to prematurely push new technologies into the marketplace — but in this context, it's a big mistake. When a new technology is discovered in the laboratory, it is the responsibility of the scientist to prove that it is safe. When this technology has the power to make substantive changes to life on earth, it is the responsibility of the government to provide a thorough risk assessment. It is the responsibility of the press to report the whole story, so that the American people can let Congress know if they think this new technology is a good direction for our society. And it is our responsibility as adults to safeguard the future for our children. So we have written this book — for our children and their friends, and your children and their friends, and their friends. . . .

Many people have asked us about our name. Our organization was born out of a simple desire — to talk to the mothers of America about natural law. Natural law is the organizing power that governs the universe. Keeping night following day, the planets from bumping into each other, mother fish producing baby fish, natural law nourishes and promotes the growth of everything, so that the universe unfolds in perfect harmony with itself. Whatever we call it, this timeless organizing principle exists and has been running the show right from the start. No challenge is too big for nature, no problem insurmountable. If we're smart, we'll choose to bring our lives into accord with its profound and effortless administration and start enjoying the support of nature's unlimited strength, intelligence and creativity in every aspect of our lives.

Our understanding of natural law comes from the teachings of Maharishi Mahesh Yogi, the founder of the Transcendental Meditation™ and TM–Sidhi™ Programs. Without this knowledge, we wouldn't have known we could change either ourselves or the world. But with it, we've discovered that life can indeed be lived without suffering, that problems melt away when the total potential of natural law is lively inside our own awareness, and that with the support of nature's awesome organizing power anything's possible. For this great gift, we are eternally grateful.

Laura and Robin Ticciati
Fairfield, Iowa

Introduction

Genetic engineering is a new technology that is changing the face of American agriculture. Touted by our government as the most exciting scientific advance of our time, the solution to world hunger and the greatest invention of the decade, genetically engineered foods made their way onto our grocery shelves in 1996. Right now, it is estimated that 60–70 percent of the foods in our stores contain genetically engineered components. The Food and Drug Administration (FDA) projects that 100–150 new genetically engineered foods will hit the market by the year 2000. These foods have not been subjected to thorough pre-market safety testing, nor are they labeled.

Throughout the world, a large and growing number of scientists, physicians, clergy, farmers, consumers, business leaders and governments are raising their voices against the proliferation of these foods into the marketplace. Seriously concerned about the potential dangers of genetic engineering to our health and the environment, as well as its inherent ethical implications, a global movement has sprung up urging that we slow down, look at the whole picture, and employ comprehensive, long-range thinking to guide the unfolding of this technology into our world.

The relationship between humans and the foods they eat is intimate. The 1960s slogan "You are what you eat," once considered a novel and controversial idea, has been proven true so often that it is now an accepted part of our world view. This makes it reasonable to ask, "Should we eat genetically engineered foods? Are they safe? Are they natural? What is genetic engineering? How does it work? Are genetically engineered foods the miracle we've been looking for to feed our planet's burgeoning population? Or do they carry with them myriad serious, unanticipated side effects and risks?"

Chapter 1

Genetic Engineering — Hopes and Hazards

Genetic engineering is a new technology that, according to its developers, was created to improve food production, reduce the use of pesticides and herbicides, and increase yields to feed our growing world population. Though the U.S. government supports the development of genetically engineered foods, many scientists believe this technology reduces the nutritional value of our foods, perpetuates our international dependence on the chemical treadmill and disrupts the flow of intelligence in the genetic foundation of our ecosystem.

Genetic engineering uses what is called recombinant DNA technology to alter the characteristics of an organism. Recombinant DNA technology is a kind of genetic surgery that enables the genetic engineer to cut, splice and recombine genes like a child building a tower out of letter blocks. A gene is responsible for a particular function or feature of an organism — e.g., red hair, blue eyes, resistance to cold. Genetic engineers use recombinant DNA technology to take the genes from one organism and inject them into another. It has been found that by introducing a gene of one organism into the DNA of another, a scientist can transfer the associated function or feature into the new organism.

At first glance, genetic engineering appears exciting, promising and unlimited in its scope. It is no wonder a scientist would want to explore the possibilities. Would you like your tomato to have a longer growing season? Well then, let's inject it with the antifreeze gene of a flounder. How about potatoes that don't brown? Or corn that can produce its own pesticide? Or soybeans that are resistant to herbicides? Or mice that glow in the dark? Or bananas that can immunize your kids? Or cows that produce drugs? Or a child that can be a great athlete? Though the imagination can certainly enjoy the vision of possibilities that genetic engineering opens up, serious questions inevitably arise. Is it safe to cross natural boundaries and create new species? What happens to the insects that feed on these new crops? What happens when the wind carries the pollen of these plants to neighboring fields? What are the reproductive implications of altering the genetic structure of an animal? Is it okay to tamper with God's creation in this way? What effect will it have as these changes ripple through our intricate and profoundly interrelated ecosystem?

Supporters assert that these questions are not appropriate because genetic engineering is simply an extension of the traditional crossbreeding that nature and farmers have been using for thousands of years. In fact, it is radically different. Crossbreeding uses natural reproductive mechanisms. Such mechanisms are only able to combine genetic material from the same or closely related species. For example, cauliflower can be crossbred with broccoli but not with zucchini. Furthermore, natural reproductive mechanisms combine the DNA of parent organisms in a very precise and systematic manner. This process does not allow a random selection of genes from one organism to be inserted into the DNA of another. The DNA of a child, for example, combines a strand of DNA from the father and a strand from the mother. It is not made by randomly inserting a few genes from one parent into the DNA of the other.

The mixing of genes by crossbreeding is clearly subject to very definite rules — you can't mix unrelated species and you can't just drop in one gene on its own, you have to take the whole package of DNA. Where there are rules there are boundaries. For example, when a donkey breeds with a mare, the crossbreed — a mule — is sterile. Nature does not support further propagation or transformation of mule DNA. Natural law has set a boundary. Genetic engineering is not constrained by these rules and crosses all boundaries set in place by natural law.

According to the Environmental Defense Fund, "Scientists can now readily shift genetic material from one species to virtually any other species. Genetic material can also be synthesized in the laboratory and then transferred into organisms. As a result, a virtually limitless number of genetically encoded substances . . . can now be added to organisms used as food."[1]

Dr. John Hagelin, award-winning quantum physicist, expressed his concerns as follows, "When genetic engineers disregard the reproductive boundaries set in place by natural law, they run the risk of destroying our genetic encyclopedia, compromising the richness of our natural biodiversity and creating 'genetic soup.' What this means to the future of our ecosystem, no one knows."[2]

Dr. John Fagan, internationally recognized molecular biologist and former genetic engineer states, "We are living today in a very delicate time, one that is reminiscent of the birth of the nuclear era, when mankind stood at the threshold of a new technology. No one knew that nuclear power would bring us to the brink of annihilation or fill our planet with highly toxic radioactive waste. We were so excited by the power of a new discovery that we leapt ahead blindly, and without caution. Today the situation with genetic engineering is perhaps even more grave because this technology acts on the very blueprint of life itself."[3]

The Dangers of Genetically Engineered Foods

According to scientists all over the world, the potential dangers of genetically engineered foods are legion. Because safety testing on these foods is not rigorous, no one knows their long-term risks, either to our health or the environment. We do know, however, that genetic engineers can neither control nor predict the effects of genetic manipulations. As Dr. Fagan explains,

> "Genetic engineers can cut and splice genes very precisely in a test tube, but the process of putting those genes into a living organism is extremely imprecise, inaccurate, and uncontrolled. Such manipulations can cause mutations that damage the functioning of the natural genes of the organism. Once a gene is inserted into an organism, it can cause unanticipated side effects. Mutations and side effects can cause genetically engineered foods

to contain toxins and allergens and to be reduced in nutritional value."[3]

So from the start, genetic engineering is risky. What other dangers are there?

- *Damage to the ecosystem, harm to wildlife and change in natural habitats.*

Our plant and animal species have evolved over millions of years. Introducing genetically engineered species upsets the delicate balance of our ecosystem with changes which would not naturally occur. Insects, birds and wind can carry genetically altered seeds and pollen into neighboring fields and beyond, creating new species. These unpredicted and unknown species may endanger wildlife and alter essential ecological relationships between plants and animals.

- *Gene pollution can never be cleaned up.*

Unlike chemical or nuclear contamination, new living organisms, bacteria and viruses will be released into the environment to reproduce, migrate and mutate. They will transfer their new characteristics to other organisms. These changes can never be recalled or contained. The effects of genetic mistakes are irreversible and irretrievable.

- *Increased pollution of food and water supplies.*

Approximately 57 percent of the research of biotechnology companies is focused on the development of plants that can tolerate larger amounts of herbicides. It is estimated that this will triple the amount of herbicides used on crops, resulting in even more chemicals in our food and water.[4]

- *Unpredictable, permanent changes in the nature of our food.*

The genetic structure of plants and animals has been nourishing the human race for millennia. Now, genetic engineers are tampering with that structure. Genes from bacteria, viruses and insects, which have never been part of the human diet, are being spliced into our food. No one really knows if they are safe. Genetic engineering is not an exact science. The new genetic structure of a plant could give rise to novel proteins in our food with unknown results for our health.

• *Deletion of important food elements.*

Genetic engineers may intentionally remove or inactivate a substance they consider undesirable in a food. This substance may have an unknown but essential quality such as natural cancer-inhibiting abilities.[5]

• *Decreased effectiveness of antibiotics.*

Antibiotic-resistance genes are incorporated into nearly every genetically engineered organism as markers to indicate that an organism has been successfully engineered. Scientists expect these genes and their enzyme products, which inactivate antibiotics, to be present in engineered foods.[6]

• *Allergic reactions.*

Genetic engineering may transfer new and unidentified proteins from one food into another, triggering allergic reactions. Millions of Americans who are sensitive to allergens will have no way of identifying or protecting themselves from offending foods. Allergic reactions can cause more than simple discomfort — they can result in life-threatening anaphylactic shock.[7]

• *Harmful effects may not be discovered for years.*

Changing the fundamental make-up of a food could cause new diseases, just as herbicides and pesticides did in the past. There are no long-term studies to prove the safety of genetically engineered foods. These products are not being thoroughly tested before they arrive on the grocery shelves — they are being tested on us.

These common-sense concerns alone should be sufficient to justify a moratorium on the release of genetically engineered organisms into the environment and food supply. However, these products have already produced unexpected and harmful results indicating that these concerns are not to be dismissed as groundless or ignorant fears.

- *Unanticipated negative ecological impact.*

A genetically engineered bacterium developed to aid in the production of ethanol produced residues which rendered the land infertile. New corn crops planted on this soil grew three inches tall and fell over dead.[8]

- *New and higher levels of toxins.*

Many plants naturally produce a variety of compounds that are toxic to humans or alter food quality. Generally, these are present at levels which do not cause problems. Combining plants and animal species in genetic engineering may create new and much higher levels of these toxins. Corn and potatoes engineered to produce toxins that kill insects are now classified by the Environmental Protection Agency as pesticides, rather than vegetables.[7,9]

- *Unforeseen and undetected toxins.*

In 1989, a genetically engineered form of the food supplement tryptophan contained toxic contaminants. As a result, 37 people died, 1,500 were permanently disabled, and 5,000 others became very ill.[10]

- *Sick and suffering livestock.*

In an early experiment, human growth hormone spliced

into pigs resulted in crippled, blind and immuno-compromised animals. Cows injected with recombinant bovine growth hormone (rBGH), have shorter life expectancies and increased incidence of disease. In addition, since the diet of most domestic animals is dominated by soy and corn, altering the composition of these crops can pose serious threats.[6,11]

What is our government doing?

Three government agencies share responsibility for overseeing genetically engineered crops — the U.S. Department of Agriculture (USDA), the Environmental Protection Agency (EPA) and the Food and Drug Administration (FDA).

The USDA oversees genetically engineered crops under authority of the Federal Plant Pest Act (FPPA). Like other government agencies, USDA must also adhere to the National Environmental Policy Act (NEPA) when they are making decisions that may have a significant impact on the environment. FPPA requires USDA to evaluate the potential impacts of the genetically engineered crop on U.S. agriculture, and NEPA requires the department to assess the potential environmental impacts of the crop. A company or other institution about to conduct field trials of a genetically engineered crop must notify USDA of its intention. To gain approval to commercialize a crop, the company must petition USDA to release the crop from its regulation under the FPPA. Many critics believe that the USDA's evaluation is inadequate to ensure environmental safety, as the department generally does not require companies to submit sufficient ecological data on the new crop to permit a rigorous environmental assessment. As you will read in Chapter 3, predicting and assessing environmental safety of genetically engineered crops is far from simple. It demands serious and thorough investigation of risk, based on ecological data derived from small-scale experiments on the genetically engineered crop itself.

The EPA has the authority to regulate certain "products" of genetic engineering under two laws: the Toxic Substances Control Act (TSCA) and the Federal Insecticide, Fungicide, and Rodenticide Act (FIFRA). Under these two statutes the EPA oversees toxic chemicals (TSCA) and pesticides (FIFRA). EPA examines only one class of genetically engineered crops — those that are engineered to produce their own pesticides (e.g., Bt crops).

(Please refer to the Union of Concerned Scientists for more information on USDA and EPA regulations. See resource section in Chapter 5.)

FDA regulations for genetically engineered foods are far more straightforward. These foods generally come under a "post-market" authority which allows the FDA to step in and force recall or withdrawal of a food or supplement if a problem shows up after the product has been marketed. In *FDA Consumer* magazine, July 1996, John Henkel writes,

> "Except for a handful of new 'food additives' such as artificial sweeteners, which must receive pre-market approval from FDA before entering the market place, most new foods are introduced under the 'post-market' authority of the Food, Drug and Cosmetic Act. Under this authority, foods made up of proteins, fats and carbohydrates with a history

of safe use in food can be sold once companies are satisfied the new product is safe without first getting FDA approval. . . . To help assure the public that this system will work as well for genetically engineered foods as it has for the 30,000 products that can be found in the typical supermarket, FDA encourages firms to provide the agency with a summary of their assessment of the food's safety and nutritional makeup."[12]

Furthermore, the FDA is only mandated by Congress to require labeling if there is "something tangibly different about the food that is material with respect to consequences which may result from the use of the food."[12]

How can the FDA justify the approval of genetically engineered products without long-term safety testing or labels? What is the thinking behind their regulations?

1. Confusing Consumers.

The FDA argues that labels will "mislead" people by implying that there is a "tangible difference" between genetically engineered foods and their natural counterparts when, according to the FDA, no such difference exists. This is a very interesting point. Let's forget for a moment all of the safety issues and focus on the concept of misleading consumers. Is there a tangible difference between Kosher and non-Kosher foods? Between products made in America and those made in Japan? A label does not offer answers to these questions but innocently provides information which helps people choose what is best for themselves. And really, where is the evidence that consumers are confused by such labels?

Labels are already full of abstruse details such as "expeller-pressed hi-oleic safflower oil," but consumers have learned how to read these labels and act on the information they provide.

The FDA suggestion that labeling of genetically engineered foods and food additives will mislead consumers is inconsistent with current labeling standards and underestimates the intelligence of consumers.

2. Honor System.

The FDA assumes that companies will be completely honest, open, ethical, impartial and competent enough to assess the safety of their own products without being swayed by economic variables.

Though there are companies like this, the practice of cutting corners to increase the bottom line is so deeply ingrained in the current corporate culture that it would be unbelievably naive to expect all (or even most) companies to uphold this high standard. According to the Council for Responsible Genetics (CRG), "The FDA has shrugged its responsibility for regulating genetically engineered foods . . . a precautionary 'safety proven first' policy has been scrapped in favor of corporate economic interests."[13] CRG continues, "If they (the companies) perceive no danger to consumers, companies are not required to state that their products have been genetically manipulated or to reveal the source of implanted genes; nor are they required to make the results of their safety tests available to the public. The FDA will not have a complete set of information regarding genetically engineered foods on the market, so there will be no way to trace who or what is responsible should a problem occur."[13] Despite documented fatalities and increased warnings from the international scientific community, the FDA claims they find no scientific evidence to support the assertion that bioengineered foods are unsafe. And they continue to maintain their current "honor system" approval process allowing the biotech industry to monitor itself, and release many new genetically engineered products for commercial distribution without thorough pre-market safety testing, advance notice or labels.

3. Substantial Equivalence.

The looseness of the FDA regulations reflects a belief that genetically engineered foods are safe. They claim that genetically engineered foods are "substantially equivalent" to (essentially the same as) their natural predecessors.

But where is the logic in this? DNA is nature's blueprint for creating the individuality of an organism. Genetic engineering manipulates an organism at the very source of its uniqueness and changes it — fundamentally and essentially. The FDA evidently supposes that the random insertion of an alien gene into an organism will cause no unforeseen changes or side effects, that adding genes to DNA will have as little impact as adding pebbles to a beach when, in fact, it could be more like adding a child to a family.

We conclude that the FDA regulations are designed to facilitate the marketing of genetically engineered foods rather than protect the interests of the consumer. As an exception, we note that FDA regulations are more cautious in the case of known allergens. "When a gene from a food that could cause an allergic reaction . . . is transferred into another food . . . FDA policy places the burden on the developer."[12]

Laura Tarantino, the head of FDA's biotechnology branch states, "The food will have to be labeled so everyone will know it contains an allergen, unless the developer can show scientifically that the allergenicity has not been transferred. . . . So this is one case where we would clearly insist on labeling."[12] But adding a gene, especially from a source never before found in human food, may introduce novel proteins into common foods, proteins which may prove to be novel allergens.

Dr. Marion Nestle writes in her editorial in the March 14, 1996 issue of the *New England Journal of Medicine,* "The unresolved status of this regulatory policy means that the responsibility for protecting the public against uncommon or unknown allergens in transgenic foods will continue to be delegated to industry and largely voluntary."[14] Clearly, the existing regulations provide inadequate protection for the consumer.

Critics of current government regulations have stated that the across-the-board fostering of biotechnology by all three government agencies will create serious problems for us and our planet — from diluted organic standards, to the growth of superweeds, to the potential loss of natural pesticides and increased resistance to herbicides, to unknown diseases cropping up in future generations. A toxicologist who has worked in one of the government's regulatory agencies for 13 years sums up the situation quite compellingly.

> "There is no process — across all U.S. federal agencies — to evaluate the hazards of GE organisms as we have for chemicals. For chemicals, we have formal risk assessment guidelines; science policies; conferences where scientific issues are debated. That's not the case with GE. We don't

even have an understanding of the full range of hazards from GE organisms. There has been no discussion of or consultation with the public to determine what constitutes 'unacceptable risk.' No method to even measure magnitude of risks.

"In the U.S., each risk assessment for GE organisms is done on an ad hoc basis by different scientists in different departments of different agencies. Some of these agencies have conflicting missions — to promote and to regulate; or to consider 'benefits' as well as 'risks.' There is rarely any formal peer review. When peer review panels are put together, they are not necessarily unbiased. They can be filled with GE proponents or confined to questions which avoid the important issues, so that a predetermined decision can be justified.

"This technology is being promoted, in the face of concerns by respectable scientists and in the face of data to the contrary, by the very agencies which are supposed to be protecting human health and the environment. The bottom line in my view is that we are confronted with the most powerful technology the world has ever known, and it is being rapidly deployed with almost no thought whatsoever to its consequences."[15]

Chapter 2

Truth in Labeling?

*"You could, in theory, select from a trattoria menu
a meal of roast aubergine [eggplant] followed by
polenta and tomato sauce, and then salmon served
with fried potatoes, followed by fruit salad — every
item, including the oil, pepper and the horseradish
sauce, having been genetically engineered."*[16]
    And none of it would be labeled.

What's on the Market?

In 1996–'97, there were nineteen genetically engineered
product sources approved for commercial distribution. As of
this printing, there are over thirty. So, hold onto your hats.
The following genetically engineered crops, all spliced with
the genes of bacteria or viruses, may already be in the foods,
supplements, household and personal care products at your
stores:

- soybeans (3 varieties)
- corn (11 varieties) — but not blue corn
- canola (4 varieties)
- papaya
- potatoes (2 varieties)
- tomatoes (5 varieties)
- yellow crook-neck squash (2 varieties)
- cotton (5 varieties)
- dairy products from cows injected with the genetically altered hormone recombinant bovine growth hormone (rBGH)
- radicchio

Several agricultural inputs, such as soil bacteria that produce the Bt toxin, and a rabies vaccine have also been approved. And that's not all. The following products may also be genetically altered or originate from genetically engineered organisms: enzymes used in the processing of cheese, candies, cookies, breads, cereals, corn syrups, oils, juices, detergents, dough conditioners, yeast, sugar, animal feed and vitamins.

What does this mean? It means that any product containing any of these ingredients or their derivatives may contain something that's been genetically engineered. Because none of it is labeled as genetically engineered or non-genetically engineered, everything we eat from one of these food sources becomes suspect. Overwhelming? You bet.

To try to get a handle on the pervasiveness of this technology in our food supply, many people have asked us for a list of foods that might contain genetically engineered organisms (GEOs), and a list of brand names that do not. We're working on it! But we face a great challenge. In the U.S., most genetically engineered crops are not segregated from their genetically natural counterparts. Due to market pressure, though, this has just begun to change. (See Chapter 5 for details.) What this means is that when the crops are harvested, the GE and non-GE versions are stored and processed together. This leaves manufacturers with the need to find out — are the ingredients in their products GE or non-GE? And if they contain GEOs, which will be the case for most processed soy and corn derivatives due to lack of segregation, manufacturers who want to keep GEOs out of their products have to start searching for other suppliers outside the U.S. When you add enzymes and processing agents (often with technical or unfamiliar names) into the equation, manufacturers find themselves with so many unknowns that they begin to feel like we do — hit by a truck.

During the past eighteen months, manufacturers all over the world have been hard at work researching their ingredient lists to determine whether or not their products contain GEOs. Trying to track down the GE or non-GE status of a product usually takes months. Sometimes there are several suspect ingredients in one product. The manufacturer must trace each one. Usually each ingredient comes from a different source. Sometimes it comes from another manufacturer or a distributor, who also doesn't know if the ingredient is GE or not. Then it has to be traced back one more level to the original supplier.

When we first began our work, we thought, as most people do, that we could just create a list of GE-free brands and be done with it. Unfortunately, as you now know, it isn't that simple.

Right now, in 1998, if you want to buy processed foods and avoid GE ingredients, you will have to read product labels, look for all of the following items, and avoid those products in which any ingredient is not explicitly qualified as organic. Here is a partial list of items you need to watch for.

• *Soybeans:*

Soy flour, soy oil, lecithin, soy protein isolates and concentrates. Products that may contain GE soy derivatives: vitamin E, tofu dogs, cereals, veggie burgers and sausages, tamari, soy sauce, chips, ice cream, frozen yogurt, infant formula, sauces, protein powder, margarine, soy cheeses, crackers, breads, cookies, chocolates, candies, fried foods, shampoo, bubble bath, cosmetics, enriched flours and pastas.

• *Corn:*

Corn flour, corn starch, corn oil, corn sweeteners, syrups. Products that may contain GE corn derivatives: vitamin C, tofu dogs, chips, candies, ice cream, infant formula, salad dressings, tomato sauces, breads, cookies, cereals, baking powder, alcohol, vanilla, margarine, soy sauce, tamari, soda, fried foods, powdered sugar, enriched flours and pastas.

• *Canola:*

Oil. Products that may contain GE canola derivatives: chips, salad dressings, cookies, margarine, soaps, detergents, soy cheeses, fried foods.

• *Cotton:*

Oil, fabric. Products that may contain GE cotton or its derivatives: clothes, linens, chips, peanut butter, crackers, cookies.

• *Potatoes:*

Products that may contain GE potatoes or derivatives: unspecified processed or restaurant potato products (fries, mashed, baked, mixes, etc.), chips, Passover products, vegetable pies, soups.

• *Tomatoes:*

No plum or roma tomatoes have been genetically engineered. But one cherry tomato has, as have regular tomatoes. Products that may contain GE tomatoes or derivatives: sauces, purees, pizza, lasagna, and all of those wonderful Italian and Mexican foods.

• *Dairy Products:*

Milk, cheese, butter, buttermilk, sour cream, yogurt, whey. You have to ask several questions when you are looking at dairy products. Have the cows been treated with rBGH? What kind of feed have they been given? If they are not being fed organic grains, chances are quite likely that they will be eating GE animal feed. What does this do to their milk products? No one knows.

• *Animal Products:*

Because animal feed often contains GEOs, all animal products, or by-products, may be affected.

Please note that a food may contain some of these items and yet be free from GEOs, but we have no way of knowing without tracking down every brand, every product and every ingredient.

Having said all of this, we have to add that, in fact, even reading labels is no guarantee that you will be able to avoid GE ingredients because manufacturers are not required to list every little ingredient, enzyme or organism used in the manufacturing process if the amount falls below a certain level.

Unbelievably, this is just the beginning. The situation will soon be much worse if the genetic engineers have their way. Virtually every grain, legume, vegetable, fruit, nut and berry has already been engineered in the lab and will enter the market in the next few years. So how do we deal with this?

If you're like the rest of us when we first heard about genetically engineered foods, you're probably quietly freaking out, wondering what on earth you can eat, whether your kitchen is full of GE foods, whether your favorite restaurant will have to be off limits, or if your local farmer's market is selling GE produce. You'll walk through the aisles of your grocery store and feel like a spy in enemy territory, searching and hoping for a way out. Should I buy this? Should I buy that? Is anything safe anymore or is everything genetically engineered?

Fortunately, there is one haven: organic foods. We know it's not always easy to buy organic. Sometimes you can't find any — and when you do they might cost more than you can afford. But if you want to avoid all genetically engineered foods, organic ingredients are the way to go. Outside this haven, you will have to become a highly discriminating label reader. Be vigilant and keep your sense of humor when your teenagers complain about the "boring" food you keep serving them!

But take heart. It is possible to cook without genetically engineered ingredients and keep even the most demanding eaters happy. Organic sugar, butter and milk provide the basis for great desserts. There are jams and spreads and all sorts of quick and easy non-GE treats available. Great organic pastas and sauces, salsas, cheeses, whipped cream, soy products and chips are tucked away on your grocery shelves. Just pretend you're on a treasure hunt instead of in a mine field. Take those teenagers along with you, and set them to work finding that non-GE junk food!

A Ray of Light—Certifying

The natural products industry is diligently responding to its consumers' desires for non-GE foods. Retailers are busy educating themselves and their customers about the lines they carry. Manufacturers are busy sourcing non-GE ingredients for their products. Soon we will see a difference — non-GE products will be available.

How will we know if something is not genetically engineered? A core group of industry members, including Mothers for Natural Law and Farm Verified Organic, set up a pilot study in 1997 to uncover and resolve all the challenges GE brings to the industry —from seed to consumer. The goal of the study was to develop viable standards for a certification process that will enable manufacturers to label their products non-GE. The foundation for this certification procedure is a highly sensitive test developed by Dr. John Fagan, scientific advisor to Mothers for Natural Law.

Though most ads depict the concept of GE foods with sci-fi combos — tomatoes with wings, fruit with fish fins, corn with insect antennae — in reality, many GE foods look and taste exactly like their genetically natural predecessors. Fortunately, Dr. Fagan's test can be used to establish definitively whether or not a particular food has been genetically engineered.

How does the test work? Since genetic engineering adds new genes to the DNA of an organism, the test is designed to examine the DNA in a food and detect the presence of those genes. For example, drop a genetically engineered soybean into a bushel of natural soybeans, grind them all up and take a sample. Then the test will look for specific new genetic material in the sample and make it visible by chemical amplification so that everyone can see for themselves that a GE soybean is in there. It produces definitive results on all raw foods and on most by-products and processed foods. The proprietary technology developed by Dr. Fagan for genetic analysis of foods has become the recognized standard for the industry in terms of reliability and sensitivity. It is available through the labs of Genetic ID, a company in Fairfield, Iowa. Corporations at all levels of the food industry contract with Genetic ID or its licensees around the world to test their products for the residues of genetic engineering.

So with any luck, we will soon be able to offer you that list of GE-free brands after all!

Non–GE Infant Formula

In 1997, Marian Burros, a journalist for the *New York Times,* hired Genetic ID to test products for an article she wrote about genetic engineering. The results of those tests showed that several commercial infant formulas (Carnation Alsoy, Similac, Neocare, Isomil and Enfamil ProSobee) contained genetically engineered organisms.[17] Pretty shocking, eh? Infant formula is presented in this country by both our government and the food industry as one of the most highly regulated, rigorously safety-tested products on the market. Yet right now, new mothers all over the globe are unknowingly feeding their babies with formula that contains GE ingredients — ingredients that have not been subjected to any long-term safety testing, have no track record and have never been tested on humans — and millions of tiny infants in every region of the world have been involuntarily conscripted into this global food experiment. To place the trust of mothers and the delicate newly developing physiologies of newborns in the path of so many unknowns is unconscionable, pure and simple.

Many people ask us why we don't simply promote breast-feeding as the obvious alternative. Unfortunately, many women cannot nurse their babies no matter how much they want to. Maybe they've had a mastectomy or AIDS. Research now indicates that the HIV-virus passes through the breast milk into the infant. Because the AIDS epidemic in Asia and Africa has escalated to an alarming level, the need for an un-infected, natural infant food source has become critical.

Locating and promoting a non-GE infant formula is a profound concern to us. Therefore, during the past year, we engaged the support of a U.S. natural products industry member to create a non-GE infant formula and are closing in on a source overseas. These options, however, may not be available until the end of 1999. We will continue our search for a non-GE infant formula so that mothers in need, wher-ever they live, will have a safe food source for their babies. Until such time, we implore the infant formula companies to truthfully label their products, so that new mothers can de-cide for themselves whether or not they will feed them to their babies.

Are We Anti-Science?

Promoters of genetic engineering often refer to those of us who question its safety as Luddites, people who oppose rather than adapt to technological progress. We'd like to take the time now to examine the relationship between science, technology and safety. We believe that the following discus-sion will make it completely clear that our vision of the po-tential hazards and recommendations for extreme caution arise naturally from a balanced assessment of genetic engi-neering and the science behind it.

Chapter 3

Science and Safety

What is Science?

The purpose of science is to provide reliable, universal knowledge about the laws of nature. Science is distinguished from other methods of gaining knowledge (e.g., religious, artistic) by its highly systematic approach — the scientific method — which matches every little advance in understanding with appropriate experimental results. Consider the activity of cooking. Everyone cooks at least a little, and most of us are not at all scientific about it. But if we want to publish a recipe, we have to measure what we are doing and provide an accurate account of it for others. It helps if we can include some explanations — bits of information such as, "Keep your freshly-made pastry cold to prevent the gluten in it from absorbing moisture and making the pastry tough." Measuring, explaining and publishing like this makes cooking a scientific subject.

Modern science is objective by nature. Objectivity is upheld because it makes experiment universal and repeatable.

For example, if we go to the Metropolitan Museum of Art one day and find it inspiring, this is no guarantee that we will find it inspiring again the next day. Our mood may have changed. We may be less receptive to the art and fail to appreciate it, or we may be more receptive and not like the way it makes us feel. Though subjective experience is perfectly valid, we do not call it scientific because it is not a useful basis for reliable, universal knowledge.

Objective experiments, on the other hand, are remarkably universal and repeatable. In principle, they make the same data about nature's activities available to anyone, anywhere, at any time. To gain reliable, replicable, objectively-based knowledge, science gathers information about natural law through mechanical apparatus which can amplify the subtle activities of nature to the point where the crudest level of the senses can tell what is happening. ("You looked flushed. Do you have a temperature? I'll get the thermometer.")

To keep further subjectivity at bay, science also tries to formulate its explanations in standardized language like mathematics. (Salesman: "This car goes a long way on a tank of gas." You: "How far?" Salesman: "Uh, over 400 miles." You: "And how many gallons?") This standardization of scientific language creates a tradition of explanations, the theories of science.

Certainly, a subjective residue persists — Newton's idea of force and acceleration was very different from Einstein's — yet the use of mathematics makes it possible to communicate the essential structure of an explanation without much ambiguity. Though the discovery of a law of nature depends ultimately on the consciousness of the scientist and can occur in any haphazard manner, the characteristic of science is the subsequent effort to state the law precisely in a standardized language and to verify the law by doing experiments to challenge this statement.

Objective Science Provides Partial Knowledge

This objective approach to science has provided a great deal of fascinating and highly reliable knowledge about the laws of nature. There is an intrinsic limitation to it, however. Being objective, it can only deal with one thing at a time. For example, apparatus designed to reveal the chemical structure of a leaf will not provide information about the shape of the leaf or about the structure of its atoms. Apparatus designed to probe the atomic structure gives no information about the molecular structure. But for the leaf to be of use to the tree it grows on, the atomic structure, the molecular structure, the anatomy, the shape and texture of the leaf must combine into a functioning whole.

Objective science can evaluate any level of structure in any object, but it cannot evaluate the holistic value of anything. This is why, for example, science cannot distinguish great art from mediocre — the quality of greatness is not found in the parts but in that wholeness which is born from the harmony between the parts. That wholeness is very real but it can only be evaluated subjectively.

Nature is like great art. It has its parts — the various species, climates, geographical conditions and seasons — and there is harmony between these parts. It is this harmony that makes the global ecosystem possible. In our bodies, it is the harmony between the organs that gives rise to individual life. When this harmony is damaged, health is damaged and life is threatened, and when this harmony is profoundly established, health is robust and life is radiant. The phenomenon of life is the indication that nature is holistic, that it manages the parts in light of a greater whole.

This managing function of nature is known to science as natural law. Scientists observe nature's performance and see that it is orderly. They investigate the details of that order and find individual laws of nature governing specific domains of nature. So we have laws of chemistry, laws of mechanics, laws of electricity and so on. The harmony between these various laws indicates the existence of a holistic value of natural law which maintains the orderliness of the whole universe.

Holistic values are abstract yet intimate. Our likes, dislikes and deep feelings are not much influenced by concrete, measurable, scientifically reproducible components of experience. They signal our holistic responses to the experience as a whole. For example, the taste of an orange is simple but abstract. We respond to it innocently without analysis. Our actions, like our feelings, reveal abstract holistic values to be more fundamental. When we see the face of a friend, we see the eyes, the nose, the smile of welcome. We do not separately greet the eyes, the nose, the smile — we greet the friend! Similarly, our favorite football team is not just a group of individual players. It is a coordinated force. That element of coordination makes the whole (the team) greater than the sum of its parts (the individual players).

Natural law, like a football team, has individual values, the laws of nature that govern different aspects of the universe, and a holistic value which coordinates all the individual laws and sustains the evolution of the universe as a whole. Since objective investigation can only study one level of one object at a time, objective science can only locate individual laws. It cannot reveal the holistic value of natural law. More specifically, the holistic value of natural law is associated with life. Life integrates subjective and objective elements. The objective approach of modern science can only provide knowledge of the objective elements. Therefore, this approach does not do justice to life, nor does it do justice to the holistic value of natural law.

This limitation applies to all sciences, including molecular biology, the scientific basis for genetic engineering. Molecular biology provides a great deal of information about the formation, structure and function of macromolecules in living organisms but it knows nothing of the organism's quality of life or its role in the environment. Of course, other sciences help to cover the territory left open by molecular biology. But even if we take all of the sciences together, our total knowledge of the laws of nature will not be complete. Knowledge of the holistic value of natural law will be missing.

Technology and Side Effects

To test a theory about a law of nature, apparatus must be built to activate that law and measure the result. This apparatus itself is a first level of applied technology based on that law. So it is inevitable that technologies develop based on the partial knowledge of natural law provided by science.

What happens when we use a technology based on the partial knowledge of natural law? When we pull the tail of a tiger it is the tiger, not just the tail, that responds. The pull achieves its purpose when the tail moves, but then there is the side effect, a hail of teeth and claws! Similarly, when technology stimulates a law of nature the holistic value of natural law responds. As a result, the technology achieves its intended effect, but this effect is inevitably accompanied by a cloud of unforeseen side effects.

Every widespread application of modern science has become notorious for side effects. Coal-powered machinery brought smog, noise and physical danger. The chemical industries have created building materials, paints, glues, fertilizers, herbicides, pesticides, preservatives and plastics — and the global pollution of our soil, water and air and a host of health issues along with them. Nuclear power brought fear of annihilation, pollution of the environment by radioactive waste, and a global wave of concern for safe use of this technology.

As technology advances, it utilizes more powerful laws of nature, and we find that it takes longer for natural processes to repair damage due to side effects. If we stop using coal in open fires then smog can dissipate in a month. If we stop creating chemicals it will take years for nature to recycle existing pollutants. If we shut down all nuclear reactors it will take thousands of years for our radioactive waste to become harmless. With genetic engineering we are manipulating the most fundamental level of living organisms. No one has any idea how nature could restore normalcy. Genetic pollution could influence life forever.

The scientist has a responsibility to society to recognize and acknowledge the limitations of modern science and carefully monitor the introduction of its applications into our world to insure safety. New technologies, no matter how exciting they may be, must be looked at with caution — time must be allowed for scientists to secure a clear understanding of all potential side effects before they are let loose in our lives.

Safety Comes with Experience

Safety is a holistic consideration. All eventualities must be considered. A scientist discovers the explosive nature of gas. Somebody builds a combustion engine. A third person manufacturers and markets a car. Now we are faced with a new device and we want to know: what are the risks? One cannot answer this question with a theoretical argument based on knowledge of the explosive nature of gas. We have to test the car itself. Perhaps it does very well on a smooth open road. If it hits a pothole, maybe the axle breaks. Perhaps a stone will shatter the windshield. Maybe a little snow will cause it to slip into a ditch. How many possibilities should we test before claiming the car is safe?

In the early days of technology, safety testing was purely heuristic. An inventor would experiment till the gadget worked, then market it. Consumer expectations were low and the cost of technological failure was less. After all, running a car into a tree at 5 miles per hour is not so bad! These days, technologies are generally quite mature and use elaborate strategies to ensure a high degree of safety. Early in the design process, risks are assessed and safety criteria are specified. When a new design is proposed, a computer simulation is created and the design is tested for safety under a wide variety of conditions. After theory has done its best through the simulation, real testing begins.

Using the example of a car, prototypes are built, crash-test dummies are seated comfortably, and the prototypes are run into walls, rolled over, sideswiped, driven at top speed till the engine burns out, slalomed through slippery obstacle courses and so on. Finally the results are assessed, and if the design passes, it is put into production. Inevitably, the experiences of new owners reveal risks and eventualities that were not tested. Sometimes a model is recalled because of a safety concern. Sometimes there are failures and the manufacturer pays the claims and apologizes, strengthens the test plan and makes the next generation of cars safer. As the example suggests, safety cannot be established by theoretical arguments. Experience alone is the practical basis for claiming safety.

The early days of every applied technology are full of disasters — medicines that prove to be poisons, bridges that collapse, steering mechanisms that fail, nuclear reactors that go out of control. As the technology matures, disasters are fewer. This indicates that test plans eventually cover most eventualities. But it takes a while to iron out the wrinkles and make a new technology safe. In the case of nuclear technology, the goal of safety has proved so elusive that responsible governments are trying to put the whole technology on ice. But whether a technology flies or dies, the basis of its safety program is applied experience carefully accumulated over time. In the case of genetic engineering, the technology is so new and the potential effects so far-reaching, there simply has not been time to accumulate sufficient applied experience. This makes it impossible to justify any broad claim of safety.

With most technologies we put up with a trial-and-error phase and allow industry to market its experiments. For example, we accept the limitations of computers and software.

We may tear our hair out when hard drives crash, but for human life as a whole, these crashes are not major disasters. We learn to back up our work and live with the occasional crash. But genetic engineering is not like computer technology — or any other technology for that matter. Genetic engineering tampers with the blueprint of life itself. It brings a level of potential disaster never before encountered in the history of technology. Clearly, these are not the kind of experiments we want to have marketed prematurely.

Genetic Engineering — Unpredictable and Unsafe

To understand the safety issue better, let's look first at the potential impact of genetic engineering on the organism itself. An organism is made up of cells. Every cell contains a nucleus. Within the nucleus is found the DNA of the organism. The DNA is an intelligence center, a dynamic storehouse of genetic material. Like the manager of a company, the DNA is sensitive, alert to every nuance of activity and information all around it, absorbing, processing and responding to the needs of the cell all the time.

Most of the structure of DNA is so little understood that it is commonly regarded as "junk" and ignored. This includes 97 percent of human DNA. Nobody has a clue what will happen if these junk elements are changed. The effects of changes may not become apparent for generations.

Genes, those segments of DNA which have been associated with specific features or functions of an organism, are the non-junk part of DNA. For example, a gene may provide chemical information which specifies blue eyes. Cellular processes turn that information into proteins, the proteins influence the chemical pathways in the organism, and the organism then develops blue eyes. Because this same process applies to every gene, the overall level of activity in the chemical pathways reflects the influence of all the genes. As a result, the expression of one gene might suppress the influence of a second gene and enhance the influence of a third. Therefore, to predict the effect of adding a gene to a cell, it is necessary to know what genes are already there, what the chemical pathways are currently doing, and what the influence of each gene is on those chemical pathways. Consideration of embryology shows how important all these factors are. In an embryo, the same DNA in different cells responds to the different conditions in those cells to guide one group of cells to become the liver, another to become the lungs, and so on.

In fact, knowledge of the organism alone is insufficient for predicting the behavior of its genes. The environment of the organism also has its effect. For example, when falling temperatures cause a bear to hibernate, its metabolic pathways take on a characteristic style of functioning and the relative influence of its various genes is changed. Indeed, the viability of an organism — its ability to survive and reproduce in a variety of natural conditions — depends on the ability of the organism to modify the degree of activity of its genes in response to changing environmental pressures.

Overall, we are very ignorant about DNA — most of it is regarded as junk, the interaction of genes is not worked out, and the role of individual genes in the overall viability of an organism is not understood. We see a vast domain of ignorance casting an ominous shadow over the whole enterprise of genetic engineering. On the shaky basis of a little knowledge, the genetic engineer sets outs to modify a living organism by adding or removing genes from its DNA. The basis for predicting the effect of the alteration is the following simple scenario:

1. The function of a segment of DNA in an organism, a gene, can be identified.
2. This gene can be transferred to the DNA of another organism.
3. The original function of the gene will show up in the genetically engineered organism.
4. Side effects for the organism and environment are not significant.

While genetic engineers may be satisfied that they can predict the transfer of a function, critics note that this prediction says nothing about the impact of this transfer on the overall functioning of the cell, the organism or its environment. Let's review the facts. Most of DNA is not understood. Genes, the little that are somewhat understood, cannot function without reference to the rest of the organism. Inserting genes into a new organism is inherently imprecise — genetic engineers have no idea where a gene will land when it is injected into a new cell. In summary, there is no basis for making a detailed prediction of the effects of genetic engineering. The successful transfer of a particular function should not be mistaken for a guarantee that there will be no side effects.

To further clarify what can and cannot be predicted, let's consider a fruit fly experiment in which genetic engineers shot extra "eye genes" into fruit fly DNA. They found that this caused extra eyes to turn up all over the fruit fly, even on its legs and wings.[18] But what happened to the metabolic pathways? To the nerves? To the fly as a whole? Is it a sick fly or a superfly ready to wreak havoc on the environment? One might predict the extra eyes and still have no idea how the organism would produce, sustain or use them. Certainly, the scientists had no idea how many extra eyes there would be or where they would appear.

The lack of predictive power inherent in genetic engineering leads to concerns for food safety. Roundup Ready™ soy, Monsanto's genetically engineered soybean, has an extra gene to help the plant resist Monsanto's herbicide Roundup™. When Roundup is sprayed on Roundup Ready soy plants, the gene is activated, and alters the chemistry of the plant and the plant survives. The manufacturer is happy because it has engineered a soy plant which can survive a dose of Roundup. The FDA is happy because the new plant is derived from a familiar crop. But what about the consumer? Obviously, tweaking the DNA has modified the chemical composition of the harvested plant. Since the behavior of the plant is novel, something in its chemistry must also be novel. Could that something be toxic? Perhaps the toxic effect only becomes apparent after five years. To summarize, the survival of the plant and consideration of the sources of its DNA do not guarantee that the plant is safe to eat.

The case of Roundup Ready cotton provides an example of an unexpected weakness in a genetically engineered crop. Roundup Ready cotton is genetically engineered to survive being sprayed with the herbicide Roundup. In 1997, entire fields of Roundup Ready cotton in Mississippi dropped their bolls or developed malformed bolls. The dropped bolls looked similar to bolls damaged by very large doses of herbicide. A spokesperson for the manufacturer suggested that the unusually cold, wet spring in Mississippi reduced the cotton's resistance to Roundup. As other varieties of cotton nearby and Roundup Ready cotton in other areas developed properly, this explanation appears reasonable — particular environmental conditions may have revealed an unsuspected weakness in the modified DNA which reduced the plants' viability.[19]

Actually, the viability of a genetically engineered crop is not at all predictable. It takes a lot of laboratory and field trials to separate viable seeds from impaired ones. So the partial failure of the commercial crop is not really surprising. Rather, it alerts us to the lack of knowledge behind the technology and raises the specter of widespread crop failure due to unforeseen environmental challenges.

To further confound the scientist, in the ordinary life of a cell its DNA is changing all the time. Genes can be marked by chemical modifications. Stretches of DNA can be rearranged, inserted, deleted or replicated thousands of times. Genes can jump from one site in the DNA to another. To understand the effect of an additional gene on an organism, it is necessary to know in detail all the ways in which DNA can change and the purpose of all those changes in the life of the organism. Unfortunately, this is too much to expect of science. But without this knowledge there is no basis for claiming that the consequences of genetic engineering are predictable.

Justifying environmental safety of a genetically engineered organism is even more difficult than establishing the organism's viability in the environment. First, the genetic engineer must learn how the novel chemistry of genetically engineered organisms will influence organisms higher up the food chain. There is little evidence of serious effort in this direction, so we expect negative side effects to show up. For example, potatoes engineered to resist attack by aphids certainly poisoned the aphids, but then ladybugs that eat the aphids were also poisoned.[20] Ladybugs are a natural control for aphid populations, so weakening the ladybug population would open the door for aphid population growth. Where does the chain end? Who develops resistance first, the aphid or the ladybug? What are the long-term effects on the ecology? Nobody knows.

Second, the genetic engineer must investigate the transfer of novel DNA from a genetically engineered organism to other organisms. For example, genetically engineered canola readily cross-pollinates with natural canola and wild weedy relatives up to 2.5 kilometers away, thereby transferring the herbicide-resistant gene to plants in the environment of the genetically engineered crop.[21] In time, this process will almost certainly create herbicide-resistant weeds and force farmers to use more toxic herbicides.

Genetic Engineering — Violation of Natural Law

In the environment, there are many organisms, each with its own DNA. Altogether, this DNA constitutes the world's genetic wealth. It is known as the "gene pool." (This term is misleading since it presumes that only the genes are relevant and the "junk" DNA can be ignored. We will use the term because it is familiar but we extend its meaning to include all DNA in organisms and in the environment.)

When Darwin proposed his theory of evolution, he did not know how individual characteristics were passed on to offspring. Mendel filled the gap with a theory of genetic inheritance — DNA is chemical information which defines an organism, and the DNA from parents combines to form the DNA in a child. As the DNA flows down the family tree, genes are transferred from parents to children. This is known as "vertical gene transfer." Though the relationship between DNA and organism is not this simple, Mendel's vertical gene transfer is one of the primary dynamics of the gene pool.

In more detail, the theory of genetic inheritance holds that the DNA of a plant or animal represents the total potential of that organism for growth, maturation, reproduction and response to environmental challenges. Any weakness in the organism reflects a corresponding weakness in its DNA. When adult organisms breed, their DNA is combined in the DNA of the child. This vertical gene transfer makes the DNA of the child a blend of strong and weak features from the DNA of its parents. In this way the DNA in the species' gene pool undergoes continuous transformation from generation to generation. The theory of evolution adds to the theory of genetic inheritance a "survival of the fittest" mechanism for refining the gene pool of the species — over time, environmental challenges eliminate the weak members of the species, thereby removing their DNA from circulation. In crossbreeding, a horticulturist or breeder gives a preferred direction to evolution by selecting parents and regulating environmental challenges. However, they leave the management of DNA to the natural process of vertical gene transfer.

It is worth noting here that vertical gene transfer contributes to genetic diversity within a species, and this helps the species as a whole to survive changing environmental conditions.

The other primary dynamic of the gene pool is called "horizontal gene transfer," perhaps because it can operate between adult organisms, a horizontal slice of a family tree. Think of the genes in the DNA of a cell as baseball cards in a collection. Consider all baseball card collections in the U.S. The collections are dynamic because people swap cards. Maybe they get together, maybe they use the Internet, maybe they put an ad in the paper, maybe they buy and sell cards by mail. The result is that by many mechanisms cards move between collections. Similarly, there is a "horizontal" movement of genes between organisms. Each mechanism, each means of movement, is called a "vector." Viruses, bacteria, fungi and insects can act as vectors in the global gene pool. Viruses and bacteria also have the ability to get into a cell, pick up bits of DNA, exchange these bits among themselves, and drop them into other cells. For the most part, each vector infects only one species, and the exchange of DNA fragments between vectors is thought to be possible but uncommon. Consequently, horizontal gene transfer will generally respect species boundaries.

Genetic engineers not only bypass conventional breeding constraints, but also dramatically extend the range of horizontal gene transfer by creating new vectors. In detail, genetic engineers use enzymes isolated from microorganisms to cut and combine segments of DNA. These enzymes make it possible to put foreign genes into viruses and plasmids, small circles of DNA found in bacteria. Viruses and plasmids are parasitic DNA vectors. They can infect cells and multiply in them. They can insert themselves into the DNA of the host cell so that they are replicated when the host cell divides. And when they do this, they carry the foreign gene into the DNA of the host cell. In short, genetic engineers have created new vectors to carry genes of their choosing to a wide variety of host organisms.

Genetically engineered vectors have three seriously undesirable features:

- They carry genes for antibiotic resistance.
- They are designed to break down species barriers so that they can shuttle genes between a wide range of species.
- They are derived from viruses, plasmids and mobile genetic elements known to cause tumors and cancers.

This means that these vectors could contribute significantly to horizontal gene transfer, thereby changing the dynamics in the global gene pool; they could provide bacteria with antibiotic resistance genes; and, though genetic engineers cripple disease-causing functions to make the vectors "safe," it is possible that the vectors will be able to restore those missing disease-causing DNA segments and become a serious health hazard.[22]

Since the combination and passage of parent DNA to the child is not a predictable process, and since the overall possibilities for horizontal gene transfer are not known, nobody has any idea how to predict the effect of new DNA on existing ecological communities. Biotech companies and the U.S. government are selling the rapid implementation of genetically engineered foods as environmentally responsible.

Given the dynamism of the global gene pool, it seems rather naive to imagine that creating super-vectors and changing the DNA in millions of acres of crops will not have serious environmental repercussions. Adding genetically engineered DNA to the gene pool could lead to herbicide-tolerant weeds, antibiotic resistant bacteria, and new dominant varieties of plants, with cascading consequences for ecosystems. The possible extent of the damage is profoundly worrying, but as it dawns on us that genetic engineers are violating natural law to irreversibly alter the chemical basis of life for all future generations, we may well come to see this technology as the greatest threat to life on earth in history. Conservative people may well feel that the whole enterprise of genetic engineering is too hazardous to pursue. Certainly, only the experience of extensive laboratory experiments and carefully contained field trials accumulated over a long period of time will lead to any realistic basis for a broad claim of safety.

Safety Testing of Genetically Engineered Foods

As discussed in Chapter 1, safety testing of genetically engineered foods is largely dictated by a concept of "substantial equivalence." This concept has been used by regulatory agencies to facilitate rapid commercialization of genetically engineered foods by making serious safety assessment and special labeling unnecessary. The tests commonly accepted as sufficient to establish substantial equivalence focus on known nutrients, toxins and allergens. However, such tests do not quantify the difference between the genetically engineered food and its natural counterpart.

With or without tests, we know that the foods are different because they were engineered to be different. The question is, is the difference a health hazard? This question cannot be answered without performing tests designed to quantify the difference. Furthermore, since the internal chemistry of the genetically engineered plant is novel and since its DNA may contain genes never before found in the human diet, adequate safety tests must include both clinical and long-term studies. (Clinical studies are ones that use people. In this case, we do not support clinical tests because we believe that genetically engineered foods are too risky to be eaten by humans or animals. We know it will be hard to find an acceptable alternative to clinical studies but we do not mind putting genetic engineering on hold until this issue is resolved.)

Consider the case of Roundup Ready soy. It is claimed that over 1,400 analyses have been done demonstrating its substantial equivalence to natural soy.[23] The manufacturer's application for market approval only provided data on concentration levels of different compounds in unsprayed beans. However, studies on Vica faba, a bean in the same plant family as soy, and on cows fed transgenic soy suggest that when the herbicide Roundup is sprayed on Roundup Ready soy, the defensive response in the genetically engineered soy leads to an increase in plant estrogen levels.[24] Thus, it appears quite possible that the sprayed beans contain a higher level of plant estrogen than natural beans. Since humans are affected by plant estrogens, this raises health issues, particularly for the use of these beans in infant formula.

Albert Heijn, the biggest supermarket chain in the Netherlands, made a marketing claim that the quality of the genetically engineered soybean "remained the same." Marketing claims, of course, are not expected to be scientific statements of fact, but they should not be misleading. The Natuurwetpartij (Natural Law Party of the Netherlands) considered the claim misleading and filed a complaint with the Advertisement Code Commission. The Commission upheld the complaint, concluding that "The quality of the genetically manipulated soy . . . is not the same as the quality of non-manipulated soy. The composition has been changed and in that case one cannot simply state that the quality has remained the same."[25]

The story of tryptophan, a nutritional supplement, reveals the weakness of the current approach to safety in genetic engineering. The problem came to light in 1989, when an outbreak of eosinophilia-myalgia syndrome (EMS) was traced to a particular brand of tryptophan produced by genetically engineered bacteria. There was no problem with the tryptophan itself. EMS was caused by contaminants which made up only 0.01% of the marketed product by weight. It appears that when the bacteria were genetically engineered to produce larger quantities of tryptophan, the concentration of tryptophan in the bacteria reached such high levels that unexpected chemical reactions produced novel toxins. The toxic tryptophan would have passed the current "substantially equivalent" test and also tests for all known toxins. In this case, 37 people died, 1500 were partially paralyzed, and 5000 were temporarily disabled.[10] To date, the company responsible has paid over a million dollars in damages. Current safety standards will not avert a repetition of this disaster.

Genetic Engineering —
A "What If?" Issue

Biotech promoters attempt to discredit people concerned for safety by labeling them antiscience, antiprogress, alarmist and extreme. It is true that the safety of genetically engineered food is primarily a "What if?" issue. What if we find out in twenty years that genetically engineered foods aren't safe after all? What if we discover some bizarre disease in the next generation that ends up linked to the oil we pour on our salads today? What if the french fries our kids devoured last week cause birth defects in our grandchildren? What if we learn that manipulating the DNA of our foods has an effect on a growing fetus after all? Or that genetically engineered foods contain some unknown allergen that produces a reaction that just can't be cured? A spokesperson for one of the largest producers of genetically engineered seeds called us to task once, saying we might as well not cross the street, because "what if" a car came at just that moment and hit us?" Our answer is, "We look both ways before stepping off the curb — don't you?"

Caution isn't extreme. It's just common sense. We just want to know — where is the research, where are the long-term studies to convince us that genetically engineered foods are safe for us, safe for the next generation, safe for the environment, safe for the world? There is an old proverb, "Once burned, twice shy." Given that our recent history is filled with misplaced confidence in all sorts of heavily promoted technologies or so-called cures that have backfired, it seems to us that we are behaving in a very reasonable and rational manner.

Chapter 4

Biotechnology Claims

Claims Versus Facts

CLAIM: Genetic engineering will feed the world.

FACT: The world can already grow enough food to feed everybody. It is widely acknowledged that, with the exception of famines triggered by war and drought, most hunger is not due to lack of food, but is caused by an inability to buy it. The immediate solution to hunger is generosity — to give food to people who have no purchasing power. The long-term solution is to foster agricultural self-sufficiency in harmony with local political, sociological and environmental conditions.

The introduction of patented, genetically engineered crops is not going to help. And to introduce technology, like the terminator technology, that renders crops sterile after one growing season is culturally, sociologically and ecologically insensitive. Indeed, it promises to bind the world's farmers to the wheel of monoculture — large areas of single crop farming — with chemical fertilizers, herbicides and pesticides. It will eliminate the small farmer entirely. In all probability, the agricultural poor will go broke and the rich who can invest in western farming technology will get richer.

The high-tech approach to solving the world hunger problem was tried during the 1960's "green revolution." Western agribusiness methods and cultivars — horticultural varieties of plants that originate and persist only under cultivation — were transferred to developing nations. At first there was the satisfaction of bigger yields. Then serious problems surfaced:

• The large-scale use of high-yield seeds required heavy applications of fertilizers and pesticides. These chemicals were both costly and ecologically damaging. They polluted soil and water and posed potential health problems to the nation, particularly the farm workers.

• The aggressive use of monoculture destroyed the diversity of local ecologies and traditional crop varieties, leading to permanent loss of crop diversity.

• The need for increased irrigation used ground water faster than it was replenished. The increased irrigation also caused soil erosion and salinization.

• After a few years, "disease-resistant" crops began to fall to infections.

• The crops were actually less nutritious — they lacked essential trace elements and minerals, particularly iron and zinc. A reduction in IQ of 10 points was also observed in the generation of children who were brought up on these foods.

Because genetically engineered crops are strongly tied to monoculture and chemical fertilizers, herbicides and pesticides, the transfer of genetically engineered agriculture will cause all the problems associated with the Green Revolution, and quite possibly aggravate them with irreversible damage to the gene pool of the native ecology.

CLAIM: Genetic engineering will reduce the use of herbicides.

FACT: At least 27 corporations have initiated herbicide-tolerant plant research, including the world's eight largest herbicide/pesticide companies: Bayer, Ciba-Geigy, ICI, Rhone-Poulenc, Dow/Elanco, Monsanto, Hoescht, DuPont, and virtually all the major seed companies, many of which have been acquired by these same chemical companies. The goal? To create companion seed/herbicide packages like Roundup and Roundup Ready soy. Here's how it works: To buy the seed, the farmer must sign a contract agreeing to use only the brand name herbicide. Since the crop is resistant to the herbicide, the farmer can use more of it. In fact, as we stated in Chapter One, some scientists estimate herbicide use will triple.[4] Furthermore, there is always a possibility that the gene which enables the crop to tolerate the herbicide will be transferred to wild relatives of the crop, giving rise to herbicide resistant "superweeds." Indeed, an experiment performed in France demonstrated that the herbicide resistance gene in genetically engineered oilseed rape (canola) spreads to wild radishes and persists through at least four generations.[26] Some of the seed/herbicide packages use herbicides like bromoxynil, atrazine, and 2, 4-D which are associated respectively with birth defects, cancer, and liver damage.[4]

CLAIM: Genetic engineering will reduce the use of pesticides.

FACT: A second major group of transgenic crops incorporates genes which produce pesticides inside the plant. These genes are generally from Bacterium thuringiensis, commonly called "Bt," a naturally-occurring microbe which produces natural pesticides. Several genes in the bacterium are responsible for production of pesticides. These genes have been used to genetically engineer alfalfa, Allegheny serviceberry, apple, broccoli, corn, cotton, cranberry, eggplant, grape, peanut, rapeseed, rice, tobacco, walnut, poplar and spruce.[27] The concern here is that crops engineered to produce large quantities of Bt continuously will "naturally select" the pesticide resistant pests, making the next generation into "superpests." A Bt resistant superpest would seriously reduce the effectiveness of Bt. Since Bt is essential for pest control in organic farming, this in turn would significantly reduce the efficiency of most organic farms. It could even threaten the economic viability of pesticide-free crops in the U.S.

The threat to organic farming is so great that a coalition of environmental, farming and scientific organizations filed a legal action against the EPA in September 1997, demanding that the EPA withdraw approval of transgenic plants carrying the genetic code from the Bt bacterium. The petition alleges that the approvals are in clear violation of federal environmental, agricultural and procedural laws.

Genetic engineering appears to be replacing chemical pesticide sprays with plants which contain pesticides. Ironically, the primary pesticide being reduced is the only natural one available.

CLAIM: Genetic engineering is environmentally friendly.

FACT: We have seen that this claim cannot be substantiated on the basis of either the limited experience available to date or theoretical arguments. But just in case there are still any doubts, here are two cases to consider.

Klebsiella planticola is a bacterium found in soil. It was genetically engineered to help dispose of wood chips and corn stalks, wastes from lumber businesses and agriculture, and produce ethanol in the process. It was assumed that the post-processed waste could be used like compost. Altogether, it appeared to be a promising package deal. When seeds were planted in soil mixed with this waste, however, they sprouted and died. Investigation revealed that the genetically engineered Klebsiella is highly competitive with native soil microorganisms and strongly suppresses activities that are important to soil fertility. In particular, the genetically engineered Klebsiella significantly reduces the population of mycorrhizal fungi in the soil. Most plants cannot get nitrogen and other nutrients from the soil without the assistance of these fungi. And of course, the genetically engineered Klebsiella continued to produce ethanol, which is toxic to plants and some microorganisms. All told, there was a significant failure to predict the adverse effect of the genetically engineered Klebsiella on the environment.[8,28]

Such failure is understandable. After all, there are over 1,600 different species of microorganisms in a teaspoon of soil. Figuring out their interdependencies is a huge task. Our point is that scientists should know that they cannot predict the effect of a new organism on the ecology and environment. They should promote serious risk assessment, safety test planning and extensive pre-release testing.

The Guardian,[29] a large British newspaper, observes that "the New York attorney general's office forced Monsanto to withdraw advertisements claiming that Roundup is biodegradable and environmentally friendly. According to the school of public health at the University of California, glyphosate [the active ingredient of Roundup] is the third most commonly reported cause of pesticide [sic] illness among farm workers." If Roundup has missed the mark of environmental friendliness, a policy of forcing farmers to use it can hardly qualify as environmentally friendly.

CLAIM: Genetically engineered foods are just like natural foods.

FACT: People have been eating natural foods for a long, long time. Indeed, nature's foods have been the basis for the emergence and evolution of the human race. So we can certainly assert that with nature's foods, we have the accumulated experience to know what is nutritious and what is safe.

Nature has organized a prodigiously complicated inter-relationship among species to form a global food chain. Every little microorganism plays its part. Every species in the global ecology has its role. The production of food, its effect on all the species who eat it, or the species that eat the species that eat it, and the influence of its decay products on the environment, are all taken into account. In order to function without mistakes, every law of nature must have complete knowledge of what is going on in its domain. The law of gravity does not have to ask about the mass of an apple. It knows, and on that basis makes the apple fall. Natural law, having the universe for its domain, has complete knowledge of everything. Nature is the behavioral value of natural law, so when Nature designs a food, it does so purposefully, gracefully, fully informed by complete knowledge.

The government says genetically engineered foods are just like those that nature makes, and the biotech industry has invested huge amounts of money to promote them as natural. But actually the biotech industry intentionally crosses boundaries set in place by nature. An insect would never naturally share its DNA with a potato. Flounders do not mate with tomatoes. Genetically engineered organisms have DNA so different it is patented. It doesn't take a Ph.D. to recognize that genetically engineered foods are not like natural foods. They are novel foods of questionable nutritional value and safety.

CLAIM: Genetic engineering is safe.

FACT: Certainly, scientists have discovered a lot about DNA. Laboratory techniques enable them to cut segments of DNA with precision. Some field trials have been done. However, the technique for inserting a DNA fragment is sloppy, unpredictable and imprecise. Neither the total effect of the insertion on the host organism nor the effect of the genetically engineered organism on the environment can be predicted. No one knows what the novel chemistry of genetically engineered foods may do to us. There has not been time to accumulate the applied experience which is the essential and practical basis of safety in all applications of science. There is no basis for meaningful risk assessment, and there is no recovery plan in case of disaster. In short, there is no foundation for asserting that genetic engineering is a safe technology with respect to food or the environment.

The Bottom Line

The obvious profit motive here belies the claims to altruism and protection of the environment. The actual activities of the companies involved reveals their true colors. Consider, for example, the patenting of food crops. If a farmer switches to a genetically engineered seed, that farmer has to sign a gene licensing agreement which specifies royalty fees and dictates the seed, fertilizer and chemicals to be used. These agreements prohibit the storing of seed for the following season. The medieval character of this relationship has given rise to the term used to describe it — "bioserfdom."

The mania for patenting has given rise to another indication of pure greed — "biopiracy" — the patenting of genes found in plants and animals in developing nations. For example, in 1994, U.S. researchers patented a hybrid variety of quinoa plant, a native highland grain grown in South America where it is an important high-protein food for millions of people. The researchers did nothing to modify the plant but now they have the right to prevent anyone else from making, using or selling that particular quinoa hybrid without their permission. Doubtless, getting permission will include payment of royalties.

One must conclude that the bottom line for biotech companies investing in genetic engineering is profit, not altruism. The *Manchester Guardian* offered the following trenchant commentary on the genetic engineering food industry:

"In a special analysis of the changes taking place in the global food industry, the *Guardian* has found:

- A revolving door between the U.S. government and the biotech industry;
- Heavy lobbying to rewrite world food safety standards in favor of biotechnology;
- New laws protecting the U.S. food industry from criticism;
- Unexpected environmental problems;
- Legal contracts locking farmers into corporate control of production;

- Attempts by the world's leading PR firms to massage debate in favor of genetic engineering;
- The use of world organizations to challenge governments opposing genetically modified crops;
- Consumers being given no effective choice of foods;
- Widespread fear that the economies of developing countries will be adversely affected."[29]

The vision of a rosy, genetically engineered future painted by biotech public relations representatives and the Clinton administration is at best science fiction, at worst fantasy. The truth is that genetic engineering aggravates the very problems it claims to solve and poses such a profound threat to the future of life on our planet that we, the people, must put a stop to it.

Chapter 5

What You Can Do

Overseas Efforts

All over the world, distinguished scientists are raising their voices to urge their governments to act quickly and place some checks and balances on the proliferation of this technology before the enthusiasm of the multi-national biotech industry for its new discovery compromises the integrity of our global food supply.

In Europe, the recent outbreak of Mad Cow Disease, a disease originating from the bizarre feeding of animal parts and offal to cows, has focused the attention of Europeans on food safety and given rise to precautionary measures regarding genetically engineered foods throughout the continent. For example, in 1996, Espoo, the third largest city in Finland, banned GE foods from their municipal dining facilities which supply 30,000 meals daily to schools and government cafeterias. Also in 1996 in Germany, the 325,000 member physicians' association (their equivalent of the AMA) issued a statement demanding the labeling of GE foods. In Austria, the government stated that it wanted to be a "Biotech-Free" zone. It took only one week during the spring of 1997 to gather 1.2 million Austrian signatures on a petition calling for the exclusion of genetically engineered foods from their country. In Norway, an act was passed prohibiting the release of genetically engineered corn, tobacco, chicory, rapeseed and pseudorabies, stating that antibiotic resistance was already a serious enough problem without adding antibiotic resistance genes into their food supply.

Great Britain has also been very vocal about the use of this technology. The British Retail Consortium, supported by EuroCommerce (the trade associations for the British and European food retail industries), took a public stand to support their customers' desires for mandatory labeling in 1997. Leading the way is Iceland Frozen Foods, the fourth largest retailer in the country, and largest manufacturer of England's frozen food supply. In March 1998, Iceland announced that its in-house product line would be made without genetically engineered ingredients, and all of its other products would be labeled. Prince Charles supported an initiative by the U.K. Soil Association challenging the rest of the British food retail industry to be non-GE by the year 2000 stating, "I believe that this particular technology is so powerful and so far-reaching that we should seek ways of engaging a wide range of people and interests in a thorough ethical debate about how and where it should be applied."[30] And the Church of England's investment fund reportedly "divested itself of shares in Monsanto because the company's genetic engineering experiments conflict with Biblical teachings."[30] In fact, the groundswell of support throughout the European Union has been so great that the Union passed a directive stating it would not accept genetically engineered imports without labeling.

The Orient and Pacific Rim have joined the groundswell, too. For example, in 1997 the leading food retailer in Japan initiated plans to label GE foods in their stores. Members of the Japanese dairy industry decided not to import cheeses that use Chymosin, the genetically engineered cheese enzyme, stating that Japanese consumers were not ready for genetic engineering. A coalition of concerned Japanese citizens collected one million signatures demanding labeling in the fall of 1997 and another million in early 1998, thereby spurring an official and organized group of Japanese Parliament members to investigate the entire issue. Similar activities took place "Down Under." "So Natural, the number two soy food company in Australia, has substantially increased (its) market share, by guaranteeing that its products were free of genetically engineered ingredients."[30] Also this year, the Australian Medical Association chairman said that "mandatory labeling was necessary to protect consumers from potential allergic reactions,"[30] motivating New Zealand and Australian government agencies to explore new labeling laws.

On the home front, genetic engineering has begun to percolate in our national awareness. The threat to the organic industry in 1997 shot the issue out of the minds of only a handful of concerned citizens and thrust it onto the front pages of the mainstream press. And people are starting to respond. Yet despite urgent pleas from scientists, doctors, clergy, farmers, business leaders, government officials and consumers throughout the world, here in the United States our government continues to rush this technology into the marketplace, ignoring or denigrating every challenge to GE — including labeling.

Fortunately, we live in a time when Americans no longer naively surrender their intellects or their trust to government or industry. The innocent faith in authority figures or "experts," once the commonly accepted norm in our society, has been so thoroughly rattled in the past forty years by shocking mistakes and coverups that the government's "Don't worry — Leave this in our hands — We know what's best — We'll take care of everything" attitude is no longer acceptable.

What's Happening in America?

Pockets of resistance have begun to form and mobilize all over the U.S. Farmers, natural products industry members, religious leaders, scientific institutes, environmental groups, animal rights activists and consumer organizations are educating themselves, conducting research, and demonstrating the strength of organic and sustainable agriculture while building coalitions and enlivening public awareness.

But genetic engineering has given rise to such a storm of controversy that even people who normally define themselves as progressive, socially and environmentally responsible thinkers and doers find themselves in a quandary over this issue. Why? Because the current administration wholeheartedly supports and promotes the use of genetic engineering as the most safe, sustainable means to feed the world. We are often questioned about this when we lecture around the country. People ask us, "If what you say is true, how come President Clinton and Vice-President Gore, well-known environmentalists, support this technology?" We can only assume that they haven't been given the whole story by their scientific advisers. We believe that if the president and vice-president could read even half of the papers that we have, they would share our concerns.

There is one point in the GE debate, however, that garners support from almost everyone, even those who favor biotechnology — the consumer's right to know. Truth in food labeling is a major issue. Whether motivated by a religious belief or health concern, the right to know generates such passion that if genetically engineered foods are not labeled, consumers will demand a change in the law. But here's what we're up against:

- Genetically engineered foods have the potential to create both a serious public health crisis and untold damage to our ecosystem for generations to come.
- During the past year, the number of genetically engineered foods approved for sale practically doubled.
- Current government regulations are minimal. Safety checks are negligible and the potential consequences to our food supply staggering.
- The mainstream press covers the pro-biotech position on a regular basis and has only begun to report the challenges raised by opponents.
- Most Americans know nothing about the issue at all.

What is Mothers for Natural Law Doing about It?

Mothers for Natural Law, once a nonprofit educational organization coordinating a national public awareness campaign on the dangers of genetically engineered foods, has returned to its roots in the Natural Law Party, the fastest-growing new party in the country, to move the issue forward in the political arena. We will continue to coordinate and support the Consumer Right to Know (CRTK) Initiative to secure mandatory labeling and a five-year moratorium on all genetically engineered foods. We serve as a clearinghouse, both nationally and internationally, for information on this issue and direct all our efforts to creating practical solutions for all the challenges it raises. Our activities are focused in four areas:

1. Consumer Right to Know–Safety First Initiative.

For the first two years of this campaign, Mothers for Natural Law served as the national coordinator of this initiative. During this time, we have created two vehicles for enlivening public awareness around the labeling issue: an ever-growing VIP list, with over 200 signatories to date, including Susan Sarandon, Paul Hawkin, Whole Foods, Seventh Generation, Wild Oats, Westbrae Natural Foods, Senator Diane Watson, Patagonia, Physicians Committee for Responsible Medicine, the Humane Society, Stephen Collins, Rabbi Michael Lerner, Mothers and Others, Gillian Anderson, Co-Op America and the Environmental Media Association. We are also spearheading a grass roots petition. Natural products retailers often serve as the local headquarters for the grass roots Initiative around the country; manufacturers, distributors, publishers and mail order catalogues are inserting our petitions in their product packaging, orders and invoices.

How can you help? Get the word out to as many people as possible as quickly as possible. We'll make it easy for you. A petition is attached to the back of this book. All you have to do is sign it and send it back to us. Duplicate it and give one to everyone you know. Or call the Natural Law Party at 515-472-2040, ext. 118.

Our goal is to obtain one million signatures in 1998. Europe's done it. Japan's done it. It's time to get America on board! It will probably take a few hours and less than $20 to make a hundred copies and distribute them. The government needs to know how we feel about this issue or policies will not change. Right now, government officials consistently tell the press that American consumers aren't like Europeans, that we are comfortable with genetic engineering and that labeling is simply not an issue in this country. We must send a strong, unmistakable message to Washington and we must do it now:

Stringent premarket safety protocols must be established before any genetically engineered organism is sold to the public. To insure that scientific rigor is upheld, these protocols must be created and maintained by an independent and professional scientific review board, i.e., one comprised of scientists who do not stand to benefit in any way from the industry they are monitoring. Until these protocols are in place, mandatory labeling of all genetically engineered organisms — from seed to table — must be secured and enforced.

2. Natural Products Industry/Organic Market Support.
One of the organization's top priorities is to protect the integrity of the natural products industry. The natural products industry has been hard hit by the influx of genetically engineered foods on the market. Take soy, for example, a staple of this industry. Because current GE and non-GE soybean crops are not segregated before processing, many processed soy derivatives cannot be found in non-GE form in the United States. This has made it extremely difficult for natural products manufacturers to keep GEOs out of their products. (Last spring, however, the American Soybean As-

sociation began to recommend segregation.This promises to smooth the way to non-GE products.[31])

Furthermore, supplements, the financial mainstay of the industry, generally contain GE components. Mothers for Natural Law works closely with natural products manufacturers and retailers to assess their specific needs, develop certification procedures for the creation of a non-GE label, source non-genetically engineered ingredients for those industry members wanting to keep their products non-GE and help coordinate a national campaign to keep GEOs out of the organic market.

Our orientation is to provide solutions which will bring strength to the industry, and position it as a haven for non-GE foods for the American consumer. We believe that as the American consumer wakes up to this issue the desire for non-GE foods in our country will parallel the desire shown by consumers throughout the rest of the world. We want the natural products industry, an industry dedicated to offering pure, whole, healthy food to society, to be able to offer non-GE foods to everyone. So we search the globe for supplies of non-GE ingredients and create a database that manufacturers and retailers can use for sourcing ingredients. We find out what they need and let them know when we find it! We also post this information on our web site at http://www.natural-law.org and offer updates on non-GE foods in our newsletters so that consumers can stay current as well.

3. Public Education.

Knowledge has organizing power. Our goal is to create a network of self-sufficient coordinators across the nation to stimulate community-based education, action and solutions. How do we do this? We have created an information packet for consumers that has been duplicated all over the world. This packet was designed to translate the science into lay language and make all consumers, regardless of their education, substantively knowledgeable about genetic engineering. We know how busy people are. We are too. So we've designed our materials to make action fast and easy. Do you want to write letters to Congress, the President and Vice-President? Would you like to let your local grocers know you want them to support your right to mandatory labeling? How about your local radio station? Newspaper? Your clergy? Your children's schools? We have created sample letters that you can copy and supplemental materials for all kinds of community activities. If your community is hosting a major event, and the opportunity presents itself, we will send someone from our national office to speak at it. Our desire is to provide enough information and simple enough action steps so that everyone who wants to get involved can do it — easily, affordably and effectively!

4. Locating a non-GE infant formula option (as discussed in Chapter 2).

For more information, or to find out how you can join in, call 515-472-2040, ext. 118. We welcome your support on every level.

Other U.S. Resources — Materials, Organizations, Action

There are several organizations and research institutions in the U.S. working on this issue. Each group has its own focus and style. The following list is included to give you the opportunity to see who's doing what so that you can decide for yourself how you would like to join in.

Pure Food Campaign

PFC is a grass roots public interest group which has been working for several years on this issue both on a national and global level to change government policy on food safety and consumer rights issues. Some of the best "street theater" and grass roots activism has been coordinated by PFC's national director, Ronnie Cummins. 218-226-4164.

Council for Responsible Genetics

CRG is a non-profit bioethics organization with expertise in several areas of this issue, including the ethics of life patenting and the responsibility of the scientist to society. Their publication, *GeneWatch,* is a wonderful reference for this issue. 617-868-0870.

Union of Concerned Scientists

UCS is a great resource for learning about the environmental and agricultural implications of genetic engineering. They publish an excellent newsletter, *The Gene Exchange,* highlighting these points as well as government regulations in this area. 202-332-0900.

Citizens For Health

CFH is an excellent resource for lobbying information and grass roots activism. They are a national organization that supports legislation initiatives particularly in the areas of natural health care therapies and consumer rights.

Consumer Right to Know Alliance

The Consumer Right to Know Alliance is an outgrowth of Mothers for Natural Law. When Mothers for Natural Law returned to the Natural Law Party, the Consumer Right to Know Alliance took over the coordination of the Consumer Right to Know–Safety First campaign. Call them for more information on how to collect signatures and enliven your community. 515-472-2809.

Environmental Defense Fund

EDF has been working on genetic engineering issues for many years. The organization has published an excellent scientific booklet about GE called *The Mutable Feast*. Call 212-505-2100, or send $10 to EDF for their *Mutable Feast* document, at 257 Park Avenue South, New York, NY 10010.

Alliance for Bio-Integrity

The Alliance is a non-profit organization inspiring Americans to stand against genetically engineered foods on the basis of religious principles. The Alliance filed an interfaith lawsuit to obtain the mandatory labeling of these foods to protect the right of free exercise of religion. 800-549-2131.

Institute of Science, Technology and Public Policy

The Institute is a non-profit educational organization founded to identify, scientifically evaluate and implement through public policy promising new technologies and programs that offer practical solutions to the problems we face as a nation. In 1997, the Institute worked closely with Mothers for Natural Law to create a national coalition of scientists, consumers and natural products industry members to protect the purity of the organic market. The Institute is an excellent resource for information on natural law–based technologies and solutions. 515-472-1200.

Institute for Agriculture and Trade Policy

IATP is an international, non-profit research and policy organization dedicated to promoting economically, environmentally and socially sustainable solutions to challenges facing farmers and rural communities. 612-870-3410.

Greenpeace

Greenpeace is an international direct-action environmental organization founded to protect the planet and all of the life it supports. The activities of Greenpeace in Europe were instrumental in bringing this issue to the forefront there. 202-462-1177.

Center for Ethics and Toxics

CETOS is a non-profit environmental group dedicated to transforming public policy to ensure technologies are safe for vulnerable and susceptible populations. CETOS offers information on alternative programs which reduce the toxic burden on society and endorses sustainable agricultural practices. 707-884-1700.

International Center for Technology Assessment

CTA is a non-profit organization assisting the general public and policy-makers in better understanding the economic, environmental, ethical, political and social impacts that result from the application of technology or technological systems. CTA advocates and represents its assessment findings concerning biotechnology in federal and state regulatory, legislative and judicial proceedings. 202-547-9359.

Consumer Policy Institute

CPI was established in 1980 by Consumers Union, publisher of *Consumer Reports* magazine, to address issues concerning consumer safety and health, and environmental quality. CPI research and advocacy seek to foster the safe, sustainable and equitable production and use of consumer products and services. 914-378-2000.

Genetic ID

Genetic ID provides genetic analysis for the food industry using Dr. John Fagan's genetic testing technology. GID is a great resource for farmers and food industry members at all levels of the production and distribution chain, who want to determine the GE/nonGE status of their products. 515-472-9979.

There are many smaller local organizations around the country working hard on this issue. Call Mothers for Natural Law to find out what's happening in your area.

How Did We Get Here?

When we first began investigating genetic engineering, we found ourselves shaking our heads in dismay. We couldn't understand why it wasn't obvious to everyone how potentially dangerous this technology was. How was it that we, a group of ordinary consumers, could raise so many questions when the scientists developing the technology were passionately extolling its virtues? How could a room full of Ph.D.s, gathered together to discuss the issue, all with access to the same facts, disagree so much? How could one government leader be certain that this technology threatened the health of his citizens when another was just as certain that genetic engineering was not only absolutely safe but also absolutely essential to feed the world? Where does this rift come from?

What is the difference between those for and those against? The answer is at once simple and very, very complex. One group views the world from a position of domination, believing that nature is something to be conquered, that knowledge of the isolated values or points of any system, e.g., a gene, a bird, a chemical, are all we need to take charge and reap benefits. The other group believes that the whole is more than the sum of the parts, that the relationships, the wholeness that's created between each part of the universe, is essential to the harmonious functioning of life itself, and must not be ignored. This group views nature not as something outside the individual, or something to be vanquished, but as the most intimate and profound value of everyone and everything.[31]

Genetic engineering is not the first technology to evoke heated debate. An entire environmental movement has grown up during the past thirty years in response to the onslaught of new technological advances that have subsequently proved to be unhealthy, unsafe, or unsound. Modern science, as we described earlier, contains within it a predilection for examining details, parts, fragments of knowledge. Though the desire to uncover, discover and understand all the laws of nature, to "know it all," is as intimate to life as life itself ("Mommy, why is the sky blue?" "Daddy, how did the apple get on that tree?"), the fulfillment of that desire cannot be gained through the scientific method. Objectivity simply isn't capable of giving us the whole picture. We forget that. What's worse, we forget that we've forgotten. And so we glorify, and pledge allegiance to, the great scientific discoveries and surrender the little niggling impulses of concern ("Are we sure that pesticide is okay?") to the rapid pace of progress. But those concerns keep coming back and some of us are starting to listen.

Genetic engineering is a global issue. The potential environmental risks travel irrevocably on the wings of insects, birds and wind across our ecosystem. The threat to indigenous species from chemical-laden farming methods, the "rewriting of our earth's genetic library"[2] through artificial gene transfer, the possibility of the birth of new viruses from the slippery fluidity of DNA are all planetary concerns that cannot be eradicated with superficial responses or sweeping brush strokes of emotional or politically expedient denial. Genetic mistakes cannot be cleaned up. They are irreversible. We believe that fact alone demands the insertion of caution, common sense and a healthy respect for natural law into our plans for the future of our planet.

Conclusion

In science, safety cannot be assumed. It must be proved by the scientist. The history of science is a history of ideas — some good, some bad, some dangerous, some benign. The experiments, research, testing, and ultimately time, pronounce the verdict. The reality is that genetic engineering is too new and potentially too hazardous for any of us — consumers, scientists, farmers, government officials, corporate executives — to be in a hurry to take it out of the labs and put it onto our dinner tables. The bottom line is that no one knows if these foods are safe for us or our environment. Without our knowledge or consent, we have all become subjects in a highly controversial experiment. At the very least, genetically engineered foods must be labeled so that we can choose for ourselves whether we will eat them or not.

Despite a recent survey by Novartis showing that 93 percent of Americans want genetically engineered foods labeled, our government not only refuses to require labels, it continues to support the biotech industry's right to suppress labels even when individual food manufacturers want to provide their customers with complete information on this issue.

The government must reverse its position. They must keep these foods out of our fields and our kitchens until they are scientifically proven safe for our environment and our families. But the government will only do this if we tell them to. So, it is up to us.

As citizens, we must take responsibility for the future. We are at a time in our world's history where we can no longer afford to violate the laws of nature in our haste for progress. We must not only acknowledge, but honor, the intimate relationship we share with everything in the universe. We need to shed our national addiction to profit-driven, quick-fix solutions and make a decision as a society to embrace technologies that support all of life, technologies that not only uphold and promote our collective growth but do not damage anyone or anything in the process.

There is an order in the universe, a seamless web that nourishes and connects us all — from the tiniest seed, to the beating of our hearts, to the stars in the galaxies. Every time we act without reference to this underlying intelligence of natural law, we harm ourselves, each other, and our planet. But if we align ourselves and our society with the nourishing power of nature, we will create a civilization that upholds the integrity and dignity of life for all of us.

Please join us.

Notes

1. Hopkins, D.D., Goldburg, R.J., Hirsch, S.A. *A Mutable Feast: Assuring Food Safety in the Era of Genetic Engineering.* New York, N.Y.: Environmental Defense Fund, October 1, 1991, p. vi.
2. Hagelin, J.S. *Natural Law Party Press Conference on Genetic Engineering,* Washington, DC, March 20, 1996.
3. Fagan, J., Joost, K., *Educational Pamphlet on Genetic Engineering,* 1996.
4. Goldburg, R.J. "Environmental concerns with herbicide-tolerant plants." *Weed Technology* (1996): 6:647–652.
5. Pariza, M.W. In *Report 2,* National Agricultural Biotechnology Council (1990): 170.
6. Food and Drug Administration 57, Federal Register 22988.
7. Food and Drug Administration 57, Federal Register 22987.
8. Hill, H.R. "OSU study finds genetic altering of bacterium upsets natural order." *The Oregonian,* August 8, 1994.

9. "EPA approves Bt corn and cotton with conditions." *The Gene Exchange,* December, 1995.

10. Mayeno, A.N., Gleich, G.J. "Eosinophilia-myalgia syndrome and tryptophan production: a cautionary tale." *Tibtech* (1994), 246–352.

11. Union of Concerned Scientists. "From the Editor's Desk." *The Gene Exchange,* December, 1991.

12. Henkel, J. *FDA Consumer,* July, 1996.

13. Council for Responsible Genetics. *Consumer Alert,* 1994.

14. Nestle, M. "Editorial." *New England Journal of Medicine,* March 14, 1996.

15. Wuerthele, S. E-mail, quoted with permission. January 1, 1998.

16. Radford, Tim. *The Manchester Guardian,* London, England: December 15, 1997.

17. Burros, Marian. *The New York Times,* May 21, 1997.

18. Nash, M.J. "Jeepers! Creepy Peepers!" *Time,* April 3, 1995.

19. Kleiner, K. "Monsanto's cotton gets the Mississippi blues." *New Scientist,* November 1, 1997.

20. Birch, A.N.E., et al. "Interaction Between Plant Resistance Genes, Pest Aphid Populations and Beneficial Aphid Predators." *Scottish Crops Research Institute Annual Report* (1996–1997): 70–72.

21. Timmons, A.M., et al. "Risks from transgenic crops." *Nature* (1996): 380: 487.

22. Greene, A.E., Allison, R.F. "Recombination between viral DNA and transgenic plant transcripts." *Science* (1994): 263: 1423–1425.

23. Burks, A.W., Fuchs, R.L. "Assessment of the endogenous allergens in glyphosate-tolerant and commercial

soybean varieties." *J. Allergy Clin. Immunol.* (1995): 96: 6, part 1.

24. Goodwin, B. et al. Third Meeting of the Open-ended Ad Hoc Working Group on Biosafety of the UN Convention on Biological Diversity, Montréal, Canada, October 13, 1997. Based on H. Sandermann and E. Wellmann, in *Biosafety* (1998): 1: 285–292, 1988, and Hammond, B.G., et al. *The Journal of Nutrition* (1996): 126: 3:717.

25. Natuurwetpartij. Press release, September 16, 1997.

26. Chèvre, A-M. et al. *Nature* (1997): 389:9 24.

27. Mellon, M., Rissler, J., eds. *Now or Never.* Cambridge, MA.: Union of Concerned Scientists, 1998.

28. Holmes, M.T., Ingham, E.R. "The effects of genetically engineered microorganisms on soil foodwebs." *Bulletin of the Ecological Society of America, Supplement* (1994): 75: 97.

29. *The Manchester Guardian,* London, England: December 15, 1997.

30. *The Manchester Guardian,* London, England: December 21, 1997.

31. Genetic ID, *GMF Market Intelligence* (1998): 19:

32. Fisher, David. Conversation quoted with permission. Vlodrop, Holland, April 7, 1998.

About the Authors

Laura Ticciati is a mother of two and the founder and Executive Director of Mothers for Natural Law. During the past twenty-four months, Laura has taken this organization out of her living room and put it on the pages of *The New York Times, Delicious!, Natural Foods Merchandiser, Vegetarian Times, Business and the Environment,* the *LA Times, Natural Health, Nutrition Science News, Environmental Times, Our Toxic Times, Conscious Choice* and large numbers of newsletters, journals, magazines and web sites published by consumer groups, natural foods manufacturers and retailers, and health and environmental organizations all over the world. Her passion for the issue, vision of possibilities and unwavering commitment to promoting natural law provide the foundation for the organization. Laura is the primary spokesperson and writer for Mothers for Natural Law, and has spent most of the past two years establishing relationships with scientists, consumers, socially responsible business leaders, food industry members and the press all over the country.

Robin Ticciati has a Ph.D. in mathematics from Harvard and has just completed a book on quantum field theory for Cambridge University Press (spring 1999). Robin has spent many years teaching graduate level courses in mathematics, physics, and the theory of science. In this context, Robin has written and lectured on the ethical responsibility of the scientist and impact of science and technology on society. He has extensive experience in systems management, database and web site development and the administration of minimally funded non-profit organizations. Robin supervises all of the research at Mothers for Natural Law, develops our public policy papers, administers all of our computer and internet projects and provides a sound scientific foundation for all of our work.

Consumer Right To Know!

Petition to Secure the Mandatory Labeling of All Genetically Engineered Foods Submitted to the President of the United States, Congress, USDA and FDA

New substances are being inserted into our foods via a technology called genetic engineering. A growing number of scientists and physicians are voicing concern over the possible health and environmental risks from engineered foods. This petition upholds the right of consumers to have the knowledge to make informed choices about the foods they eat and feed their families—and will monitor the safe unfoldment of genetically engineered organisms into our food chain.

We, the undersigned, as citizens of the United States of America, strongly urge the passage of legislation and policies to mandate the clear and accurate labeling of all foods derived from, processed with, containing or consisting of genetically engineered organisms or agricultural application which affects the food supply—and a minimum five-year moratorium on the release of any further genetically engineered organisms into all levels of our food chain—from seed to processing to table—until adequate safety protocols can be put into place to assess their risk to our health and the environment.

Name	Phone	
Street		
City	State	Zip

Name		Phone	
Street			
City		State	Zip

Name		Phone	
Street			
City		State	Zip

Name		Phone	
Street			
City		State	Zip

Name		Phone	
Street			
City		State	Zip

**Please make copies of this petition and give them to
everyone you know. Collect as many signatures as possible
and mail completed petitions to:**
Mothers for Natural Law, P.O. Box 1900, Fairfield, IA 52556
Tel: (515) 472-2040, ext. 118   Fax: (515) 472-2011
www.natural-food.com
The Natural Law Party of the United States of America

Index

agribusiness, 46
allergens, 6, 13
allergic reactions, 6, 12
Alliance for Bio-Integrity,
    64–65
American Soybean Associa-
    tion, 60
anaphylactic shock, 6
animal feed, containing
    GEOs, 19
antibiotic-resistance, 6, 40
aphid-resistant potatoes, 37
atrazine, herbicide, 47
Australian Medical Associa-
    tion, 56
Austria, "biotech-free" zone,
    55

bacteria, antibiotic resistant,
    41

Bacterium thuringensis (Bt),
    47
  crops, 9
  toxin, 16
biodiversity, 3
"biopiracy," 52
"bioserfdom," 52
biotech industry, 70
  lobby, 52
biotechnology fostering, 13
British Retail Consortium, 55
bromoxynil, herbicide, 47
Burbank Russet potato, 18
Burros, Marian, 22

cancer, and herbicides, 47
canola derivatives, 18
Carnation Alsoy, 22
Center for Ethics and Toxics
    (CETOS), 66

chemical industry, 29
chemical pathways, 33
Church of England, and Monsanto shares, 55
Chymosin, 56
Citizens for Health (CFH), 63–64
clinical studies, alternatives to, 42
Co-op America, 59
coal-powered machinery, 29
computer simulation, safety, 30
Consumer Policy Institute (CPI), 66–67
Consumer Reports, 66
Consumer Right to Know Initiative, vii, 58, 59, 64, 75–76
Consumers Union, 66
corn
  derivatives, 18
  GE, as pesticide, 7
cotton, GE, 18
Council for Responsible Genetics (CRG), 11, 63
crash-test dummies, 31
crossbreeding, 2, 38
cross-pollination, GE canola, 37

dairy products, GE, 19
Darwin, Charles, 38

database, non-GE ingredient sources, 61
diversity, genetic, 39
DNA, 2, 3, 21, 32, 33, 36, 38, 50
  fragment insertion, 51
domination world view, 68

ecosystem, 2, 3, 69
  damage to, 5, 41
embryology, 33
Enfamil ProSobee, 22
environmental assessment, 8
Environmental Defense Fund (EDF), 3, 64
Environmental Media Association, 59
Environmental Protection Agency (EPA), 7, 8, 9
environmental safety, GEOs, 36
environment, effect of on organism, 33
enzymes, 39
eosinophilia-myalgia syndrome (EMS), 43
Espoo, Finland, ban on GE foods, 54
estrogens, in GE soy, 42
EuroCommerce, food retail, 55
evolution, theory of, 38
"extra eyes," fruit flies, 34–35

Fagan, John, 3, 4, 21, 22, 67
FDA Consumer, magazine, 9
Federal Insecticide, Fungicide, and Rodenticide Act (FIFRA), 9
Federal Plant Pest Act (FPPA), 8
fertilizers, 46
field trials, 8, 51
food chain, 37, 50
Food and Drug Administration (FDA), xi, 8, 9, 10, 11, 12
Food, Drug and Cosmetic Act, 9
food safety, 54
fruit fly experiment, 34–35

Gene Exchange, The, 63
gene licensing agreement, 51
gene pollution, 5
gene pool, 37, 38
genes, 1, 32, 33, 36
GeneWatch, 63
genetically engineered organisms (GEO)
    crops, storage and processing of, 17
    products available, 16
genetically engineered (GE) vectors, undesirable features, 40

genetic engineering (GE)-free brand list, difficulty of creating, 17
Genetic ID (GID), 22, 67
genetic inheritance, theory of, 38
genetic pollution, 29
"genetic soup," 3
genetic testing technology, 21–22, 67
global gene pool, and horizontal gene transfer, 40
global pollution, 29
glyphosphate, 49
Great Britain, mandatory labeling, 55
Greenpeace, 65–66
"Green revolution," 46
Guardian, The, 49

Hagelin, John, 3
harmony, 26, 27
hazard evaluation, of GEO, 13–14
herbicide-resistant weeds, 37, 41
herbicide tolerance, 5, 47
herbicides, 1, 6, 13, 46, 47
high-yield seeds, 46
holistic value, 26, 27
honor system, product safety, 11, 12

horizontal gene transfer, 39
human growth hormone (HGH), 7–8
hunger, 45

Iceland Frozen Foods, non-GE foods, 55
individual laws, 28
infant formulas, commercial, 22
ingredient lists, manufacturers, 17
Institute for Agriculture and Trade Policy, 65
Institute of Science, Technology and Public Policy, 65
International Center for Technology Assessment, 66
Isomil, 22

Klebsiella planticola, 48–49

label, non-GE, 61
labeling, 16, 19, 70
    demand for in Japan, 56
    mandatory, vii, 10, 55, 59, 62, 75–76
    support for in Great Britain, 55
lady bug, natural aphid control, 37
long-term risks, 4

long-term studies, 6
luddites, 23

Mad Cow Disease, 54
Maharishi Mahest Yogi, ix
Manchester Guardian, 52
mathematics, 25
Mendel, Gregor, 38
molecular biology, 28
monoculture, farming, 45, 46
Monsanto, 35, 47, 49, 55
Mothers for Natural Law, vii, 21, 22, 58, 61, 77
mule, sterility of, 3
Mutable Feast, The, 64
mutations, 4
mycorrhizal fungi, 49

National Environmental Policy Act, 8
natural habitats, change in, 5
natural law, ix, 3, 27, 50, 69, 71
Natural Law Party (NLP), 64
Natural Law Party of the Netherlands (Natuurwetpartij), 43
natural pesticides, 48
natural products industry, 21, 57, 60
natural reproductive mechanisms, 2
Neocare, 22

Nestle, Marion, 13
New England Journal of Medicine, 13
New York Times, 22
non-GE certification, 21, 61
non-GE infant formula, 22, 23, 62
Norway, prohibition of GE products, 55
Novartis, 70
nuclear power, 4, 29

objective experiments, 25
objectivity, 24
oilseed rape. *See* Canola
organic farming, threat to, 48
organic foods, 20

Passover products, GE, 18
peer review panels, GEO, 14
pesticide oversight, 9
pesticide production, and Bt, 48
pesticides, 1, 6, 13, 46, 47–48
petition, 59, 78
plant estrogens, 42
plasmids, 39
"post-market" authority, 9
potatoes, GE, 18
    aphid resistant, 37
    as pesticide, 7
pre-market approval, 9

pre-market safety testing, 12, 60
proteins, 33
public relations, biotech industry, 52, 53
Pure Food Campaign (PFC), 63

quinoa plant, 52

rabies vaccine, genetically engineered, 16
radioactive waste, 29
recombinant bovine growth hormone, (rBGH), 8, 16, 19, 76, 77
recombinant DNA technology, 1
reproductive boundaries, 3
review board, scientific and professional, 60
Roundup Ready™ cotton, 35–36
Roundup Ready™ soy, 35, 42, 47
Roundup™ herbicide, 35, 47, 49

"safety proven first" policy, 11
safety testing, xi, 4, 41
    heuristic, 30
    holistic, 30

salinization, 46

scientific method, 24

Similac, 22

single crop farming, 45

soil erosion, 46

soybean
   GE, in Netherlands, 43
   processing, 60
   products, non-organic, 18

species boundaries, gene transfer, 39

standardization scientific language, 25

"street theater," 63

subjective experience, 25

substantial equivalence, 12, 41

"superpests," 48

superweeds, 13, 47

"survival of the fittest," 38

"tangible difference," 10

theory, testing, 28

TM-Sidhi™ Programs, ix

tomatoes, GE, 19

toxic chemical oversight, 9

Toxic Substances Control Act (TSCA), 9

toxins, 7

Transcendental Meditation™, ix

transfer of function, 34

transgenic foods, 13

trial-and-error phase, 31

truth in food labeling, 58

Tryptophan, contaminated, 7, 43

2,4-D, herbicide, 47

U.K. Soil Association, non-GE foods, 55

U.S. Department of Agriculture (USDA), 8

"unacceptable risk," GEO, 14

Union of Concerned Scientists (UCS), 9, 63

vectors, 39, 49

vertical gene transfer, 38, 39

viability, GE crops, 36

Vica faba, bean, 42

viruses, 39

vitamin C, with GE corn derivatives, 18

wholeness, world view, 68

wildlife, harm to, 5

wild radishes, 47

Wuerthele, Suzanne, 13